A Knuckle-Deep Ocean

BABAK ESMAEILY

A Translate by : Bijan Safshekan
Cover Designer : Shabnam Saveyi

authorHOUSE®

AuthorHouse™
1663 Liberty Drive
Bloomington, IN 47403
www.authorhouse.com
Phone: 1 (800) 839-8640

Published by AuthorHouse 08/07/2018

ISBN: 978-1-5462-5319-8 (sc)
ISBN: 978-1-5462-5318-1 (e)

Print information available on the last page.

This book is printed on acid-free paper.

Special thanks to:

Dear Amanda and Greg Oppenhuizen, Dear Tim and Brigitte Brenda, Miry's list and Eagle Rock neighborhood, Dear Miry whitehill, Dear Mahin and Ali and Ghazal Bazrafshan, Dear Shirindokht Daghighian, Dear Danielle and Dan Cota, Dear Ahlems, Dear Elizabeth and Jonathan Hogan, Dear Narjes Zare, Dear Maria Guadalupe Garibay, Dear Solmaz and Reza Qolizadeh, Dear Majid Aliei, Dear Bijan Safshekan, Dear Shabnam Savei, Dear Elham Nikfarjam, Dear Meliha Ezer, Dear Husnu Murat Aydin, Dear Partow Nouriala, Dear Daniel Lemke, and Dear Dustin

Dear Jay and Kristi Fiorini who did not start the translation process without them.

Dear William Overman, April Roma and Other guys in Author House.

To My Dear Behniya
Forgive but do not forget

Life in West Aban Alley

Mom had woken up and started making noises since six in the morning. She dropped the pot once; scattered the forks and spoons on the floor a couple of times; and I would cover my head under the blanket, so I wouldn't hear the noises. This was my father's way to wake us up. He'd make so much noise every morning that you'd have to wake up. It was seven in the morning when mom called a friend and put it on speaker. I, again, covered my head and ears under the blanket so I wouldn't hear the noise. Then, until seven thirty, she called me a couple of times: Get up. Aren't you going to Tehran? Get up, it's late.

I hate getting up early and disturbing my sleep for apparently important matters. These days, there's nothing so important in my life, for which I'd get up early. Why getting up has to be more important than sleeping to me. Why going to Tehran and joining the bidding has to be more important than the comfort of my bed. What do I achieve if I change the order of my priorities? Importance. However, can something gain importance to me? In Iran, time is not important at all. Unlike my youth, it's been a long while that I've been living like Californian native Indians who didn't know their ages. Everything had been so important to me until some years ago. Punctuality, for instance, or doing things in shorter time. Details were as important as totalities to me. Doing things as soon as possible, isn't necessary to me. I don't know what such approach will cause in me and life. I won't quit doing the things I like for some nonsenses which matter to others.

By the government's order, for three days, the whole country shuts down suddenly and with no warnings. The post office delivers the mails and letters in ninety-six hours instead of forty-eight. To reply an email, you must wait for two or three days so the connection might be fast enough to open Yahoo or Gmail. The prices might be raised up to two or three or a hundred times overnight. The streets go one way without notifications. So, to get to your destination you must stall in traffic for an hour. In such situations, the stupidest thing was to get angry with someone who's late, which I would.

Many years earlier I'd been executive director of a multifunctional institute. There was a couple of days before the book fair opening and my colleagues and I wanted the book, editing of which was almost over, to make it to the fair. The writer lady worked twenty-four hours on the last day to finish the editing. When she finished working she started crying. "My father is so mad because I've been out for two nights" she said. Editing and typography and cover design were done simultaneously, and I'd had one of the biggest printing offices in Tehran do the printing procedure. Those days, lithography was done manually and there were no signs of any digital printing machines in Iran. The eve of the day, when I was going to send my 400-page-book to the printing office, the manager called me saying that there'd been a big explosion on electricity box and they couldn't accept any books to be printed for the following days. The same night I called one of my friends, who was a lithographer, and told him about the problem. It would take 3 days and nights to lithograph a 400-page-book. I had enough time to find another printing office. I talked to hundreds of printing managers on the phone the next day. It'd take at least a week for a printing machine to get vacant for a new book. We'd lose the book fair anyhow.

In the evening of the same day I explained the problem to my colleagues. And one of them explained it to his students. "My uncle is manager of a governmental printing office" one of the students had said. The girl called her family that very moment and an hour later the printing office manager promised to prepare two machines, so the book would be printed in a day. I decided to help the lithographer preparing everything needed so it'd be faster. I asked one of the colleagues to go to the printing office, electricity system of which was broken, and transfer our papers to the new office early in the morning. We were supposed to get to work at 9 in the morning. I took some of the prepared stuffs to the office at 8 and waited for the papers. The papers arrived at 12. "I can't keep the machines idol for too long, or else I'll be reproached because it's a governmental place" the manager had told me earlier. The printing was postponed to three days later and we lost the book fair. I was like a ball of fire for a couple of days. All my overnight work, the writer, the typist and the lithographer's, were in vain for my colleague's oversleeping. After I had taken a severe revenge on my colleague, with whom I was a good friend, during the directors meeting, I never assigned him to any more important thing. I didn't take him serious anymore. Gradually our relationship faded away. It's been a long time now that I've quit such attitude. If today I am to see someone, I go to see them perhaps next week or if today I am to see someone at 5, I might see them at 5 but some days later.

Last night I wanted to watch a movie which would finish at midnight. The movie happened to portray a man who resembled me so much and after a long time, I mean ten or twelve years, I was seeing myself in a movie, and I liked it. I'd seen myself last time in the movie "The Eighth Day". A man who other than work, had left himself with nothing. This time, the movie portrayed a lecturer man who had a personal philosophy. He had no commitments to anyone or anything. No relationship or attachment; which was why he wasn't married. It was him with a suitcase. He met a woman who was like him in the middle of the movie and they spent a couple of days together. A while later he decided to go to the woman. He'd fallen in love with her. He left in the middle of a lecture. When he got to the woman he found out that she was married and had two children. The woman told him that he'd been a break in her real life. The man was left alone with his philosophy. After that I watched another movie. I was up till the very morning. In such situations, my mom insisted that I'd wake up, but I preferred to sleep.

There's no reason I shouldn't live the moment. For years, I used to plan for even drinking water. I wouldn't do or say anything without an arrangement. But since I figured life goes on more fluidly with no care, I'm living for whatever happens. With no relationship or attachments, or any commitments to anyone or anything. I gradually quit everything until I reached this point. Nothing matters to me. Every work or thought or decision is either made or done or thrown away at the moment; even writing. I've thought about how to begin and keep on my story or novel many times. I've planned and puzzled for a new novel once or twice, every time though, I preferred to leave writing to my subconscious.

5

Then while rewriting I can make some changes if I'd like to. I can also keep the original text if I want to. Nowadays, my all moments are overflowed with creativity.

It was seven thirty in the morning when Hana who'd left for school rang the bell. The gong-like sound of the bell sent chills down my spine. It's been years that bells exasperate me. When I was younger, once when I was going to work in the morning and had dressed up and drunken my tea and gotten ready to leave, as usual, like modern couples, I went to the bedroom to kiss goodbye the woman who was my wife those days. To my astonishment, she burst into tears once she saw me. She said she'd been lonely, and I hadn't paid her enough attention. That day I was sitting by the bed in my suit talking to her for two or three hours. Then the phones went off. I've been running away from every phone ring ever since. I had hundreds of phone calls from work that day. It was hilarious. I'd stay home not to go to work, but work would come home through the phone. I fought everyone at work the next day. They couldn't make decision without me. Since then, I cut off the landline at home. There was no phone at home for some years. We also executed the rehabilitation program of the staff and directors, so they could deal with the matters which would arise, while I wasn't around. Every phone rings or any rings similar to them distresses me ever since.

The bus apparently hadn't turned up and Hana had asked mom to give her a ride. This also was one of the usual plans. Every time the bus doesn't turn up, my mom gives Hana a ride to school. I, again, covered my head under the blanket and frowned. If it was twenty years ago, I'd get angry, but now, it's been years that I don't get angry. I wanted to say that I wouldn't go to Tehran. You go. Screw the university. Eventually I quit sleeping with all the noises, took a shower and wore my suit. My mother, who'd already given Hana a ride, also got ready. We went from Karaj to Tehran and arrived at the university. I showed the secretary the letter which I'd written to the dean. "You need to go to the bureau department" the secretary said. We moved again. Through Jannat Abad we reached Martyr Bakeri Express Way. Tehran in now full of Express Ways under the war martyr's names. Hemmat, Bakeri, Sattari, Abshenasan. We'd followed the address I had in my hand, all the way to the end; up to a square called University Square. There were some high-rise buildings around the square.

There was a tall girl walking down the sidewalk. I thought she might be a student and knew the university buildings. I pulled over and gave her the paper. "You should go…" she read the first line and said. "Read the last line" I said. She read it again. Every time she looked, her eyes were full of intimacy which she should have left to me and gone. There was something in her eyes which would drag me towards her. "Over there" she raised her hand and pointed. She gave me back the paper and left. I again called her and asked her to show more accurately. She'd speak through her eyes. "Over there" she raised her hand again. After a short pause, she called my mother's name. My mother didn't know her either. "You?" We asked. "I am Dena" she answered. I searched my mind but there was no Dena there. My mother suddenly got off the car and hugged her. I guessed it must have been one of her friends. A beautiful woman with a delicate body and delightful eyes. "So introduce us so we'd get acquainted" I said. "We were neighbors" the girl said. "Long ago…" mom said, and I recalled. "How did you recognize us?" I asked. "I recognized both you" she told my mom. I'd last seen her nearly twenty years before. Last time I was sixteen and Dena was eight or nine. Glamorous with her hair like an ear of wheat when dancing with the wind. We'd been neighbors for about seven years. Not next-door neighbors though. We lived in the same alley. Neda was my younger sisters' play mate. I was thrown back to my childhood; in an alley called West Aban. A time, part of which there was war. A time, most important feature of which was love being forbidden. No girl was allowed to talk with any boy. Any kind of companionship amongst boys and girls was forbidden and in case of being seen together, they'd get arrested; or if the family figured it out, the girl would get beaten and the boy had to flee not to get killed. A time when boys would ambush women getting in a taxi or on a bus, to see their bare legs. The 60s… (1980s)

In West Aban Alley there lived diversity of cultures; with odd names which I got to know once we settled there. Kazem, Nader, Saeed, Sadegh, Habib, and many more names like those. In an alley on the wall of first house of which was written, by paint, West Germany, there lived Azari and Lor people, and others from Fars, Isfahan, Semnan, Yazd, Rasht, Qom and Khoozastan.

On the first week, when we'd just moved in and I didn't know any of the other kids, there was a street soccer game competition, and as always, soccer became the reason for friendship. Every evening, some women in linen bright chador would gather at a doorstep and talk or clean out the vegetables. Girls in chadors or headscarves would gather at another doorstep and whisper and giggle. The younger ones would play hopscotch and adolescents would play soccer, or Haftsang and Alakdolak (Iranian games), or hide and seek. I was passing my secondary school. A three-year-period between the five-year primary school and the four-year high school. It was wartime. The heats generally would work on either oil or gasoline. Gas was distributed in metallic capsules and the food was cooked on oil consuming stoves. For necessary items there were coupons, in other words, they were rationed. The neighbors in West Aban Alley, would spend a long time in a line for oil every week. An oil tank truck would turn up every week, and after receiving the coupon would give a 20-liter-barrel of oil to each family. Rice, milk, cookies, eggs, chicken, beef, razor, soap, detergent and in fact all necessary and unnecessary items had been rationed. Vegetables, fruits, bread and black cloth for sewing chadors were the only non-rationed items. Banana, which was a highly consumed fruit until early after the revolution, was absent among other fruits even long after war finished. Pineapples also were history. An epic had to be created to get bread. It was like there was only one bakery for every one hundred thousand people. It'd take a couple of hours to get bread. There usually were three parallel lines, one for men, one for women, and the other one for those who wanted only one bread. Those, whom you could see always and in a large number in the lines, were Afghans. Those years, Iran was a refuge for Afghans who had to flee their country due to the civil war and Russians invasion. I didn't like Afghans, because of the huge lines they'd make at the bakery and the large number of bread every one of them would get. Normally every one of them would get ten to twenty loaves of bread at each turn, and this amount almost equaled half of the whole bread which one tandoor would make; and also, it equaled consumption of three or four families in a day.

Those days, unlike my father, I didn't have a proper understanding of the Afghans' situation. They'd do anything for money, and I didn't really know that belligerent Iran was their safe haven, and Barbari bread, which back then cost two Tomans, counted as immigrant Afghans' almost whole food. I was afraid of them, yet my father would behave them respectfully. Afghans usually lived and worked in groups. There were hardly any conversations between them and Iranians. Perhaps the high rate of crime was one of the reasons. Back then, there was no day that the troubles Afghans made, wouldn't hit the headlines. Murder of a whole family, burglary etc. almost all crimes were committed by Afghans or ended up with their names tagged on them. "Most of these people, don't want to kill neither the Russian soldiers nor their fellow Afghans." My father would say. "They are decent people who's had to immigrate. Now they're our guests. We're not in a position to help them, at least we can behave them respectfully."

The relationship between the families living in West Aban Alley was spectacular. One would borrow a meat masher from a neighbor to mash the cooked ingredients of their Gooshtkoobide (an Iranian food resembling Pâté), then they would return it along with some of their food wrapped with bread. The other one would borrow kabab skewers and onions from the other neighbor, then would come back with two or three kababs and grilled tomatoes and lavash. Borrowing headscarves and manteaus and suits for fancy gatherings were also the neighbors' routine. Some neighbors in our alley had VCRs. Having VCRs, however, was forbidden, let alone having videotapes, which were traded or rented underground. Most nights, the neighbors would gather in a house, shut the curtains and altogether would watch a movie. If the cops figured that there was a VCR in a house, they'd enter the house with no warrant and take the movies and the VCR and its owner away. Lending or owning movies were serious crimes when they'd forcibly draft the youngsters to go to the war. However, love of cinema would pale our fear. Every Friday eve (weekends), along with some other kids, with whom we didn't have anything to do but playing soccer, we'd go down a long way to rent a couple of movies; 007 Agent, Sangam, Sholay, Mamal Amrikayi (American Mamal) and dancing and singing shows which no one knew how they would reach Tehran all the way from Los Angeles. Every now and then, a guy who owned movies and sold or rented them, would get arrested; and when we went to his doorstep, he either wouldn't open the door or through the half open door would say: "go away and never come back here". I saw one of the movie renters a while after he'd gotten arrested and released. He told me that they'd seized all his stuffs beaten him so much that he'd passed out a couple of times. In the last course of torture, to teach him a lesson, one of the guards kicks his penis, he bends over in pain and the other guard, wearing pointy shoes, kicks his anus saying: "our kids are dying defending our country then you rent movies you asshole?" They send him to the hospital and since they get afraid of his high rate of injuries, they release him. From then on, he couldn't walk. His testicles were so swollen that he had to have his pants sewed and because of his everlasting pain he'd always walk bending forward. The more advanced the police became, the more skilled the smugglers got. Every once in a while, they'd go to their old customers unexpectedly and hand over the movies there.

The 60s (1980s) had another distinctive specification: Pederasty. The crimes committed regarding this is a sealed mystery. Most of the news concerning raping boys was about Afghans. It was like once they found a boy alone, they'd engage. But it wasn't only them. Pederasty was also common in and out of schools. Apparently, a generation had still remained from Sodom and Gomorrah. No organizations or individuals ever, focused on sexual abuses like those. The memories have been buried under the most hidden layers of the victims' minds. At boys schools, talking about their experience by those who'd screwed younger boys, was so common and the words would be spread through classes. Such relationships had become so ordinary that there were conversations about it everywhere, and no one would do nothing about it. The matter was way beyond homosexuality. "When there are limitations, there's always a way to satisfy your instincts." The youngsters would say. The same way Lot's daughters found a way after destruction of Sodom and Gomorrah. One day the older daughter said to the younger, "Our father is old, and there is no man around here to give us children, as is the custom all over the earth. Let's get our father to drink wine and then sleep with him and preserve our family line through our father." Old Testament, Genesis.

My friendship with the kids from the new neighborhood formed quickly. Saeed was a mediocre student. He was the only son in an eight-member-family. His father was a short man with a protruding belly and a large mustache. He never looked at kids directly in the eyes, like you would think he didn't even see them. He didn't say hi back to kids either. Saeed's father had married his second wife shortly before we move to

West Aban Alley and the other kids, occasionally would talk about Saeed's parents' quarrels. About shattering glasses in their house. The man would draw a knife and threaten to kill his woman. Or the mother would pick a knife to slit her own throat. Eventually, all the fightings end up with Saeed's father marrying the second wife. Saeed, on the other hand, would swear in front of the other kids, that someday, he'd take his mother's revenge on his father and the second wife. Those days there was no books in the family's shopping basket. It wasn't rationed either which if it was, it would be so good, and we'd figure earlier that in such cases we must not think about revenge. I, though, had some books: Little Red Riding Hood, Puss in Boots, Hansel and Gretel, etc. and a grand Diwan-e Hafez with glossy papers illustrated by Mohammad Tajvidi's Persian paintings which was like a treasure to me. There were Golestan and Bustan-e Saadi next to Rubáiyát of Omar Khayyám at our home too. The only Diwan-e Hafez available in West Aban Alley was my book and occasionally was referred to in order to extract some lyrical poems for some purposes. Saeed, every day, would come up to me with his new plans for revenge, then we'd complete his plans but eventually we'd conclude that it wouldn't work. Years later, when we moved out of West Aban Alley, Saeed still hadn't managed to revenge the way he liked it.

In West Aban Alley Kazem was known as Bruce Lee because he'd bitten the other guy during a street fight when he was a kid. He was proud of his title. Because of his low grades in his lessons he got beaten by his parents and teachers so much that he quit studying entirely. A while later he found a job. Marquetry. Woodcarving. For a long while Kazem was the good kid of the neighborhood. He'd dress up fancily and, in the evenings, when he was back from work, would tell us, who were back from school, about things that had happened at his work. Saeed, Kazem and I had a good and close relationship with the two-member-gang of Nader and Morteza. There were a couple of other kids who were older than us and they either would go to work or were fugitive conscripts. Apart from saying hi, we didn't have anything to do with them. In other words, we would take the younger ones for granted. Nader and Morteza, also, failed at school so many times that they had to take up second education and after a while they quit studying. In studying competitions, Saeed and I were the oldest.

The girls from West Aban Alley were also growing up one after the other. The first one to go to high school was a girl called Leyla who'd been spotted walking with a boy from West Dey Alley, on the way to school. Saeed and I, after hearing the news, beat the boy up. Poor thing would swear that he hadn't harassed Leyla, and it'd been first her to send him a letter. Saeed and I committed every crime while we were together. We'd skip others in the line to buy bread. We'd stall in the alley and have ice cream in middle of winter when it was snowy. We'd play street soccer to death. We'd send letters to the girls who weren't from West Aban Alley. We'd stall in the alley in Chinese white sneakers and black shirt and pants. We'd talk about our loves and write heart-melting lovely letters to our beloved ones, with whom we hadn't talked even once; even though we wouldn't dare to send them the letters. Everything was normal until a summer, when a girl whose name was Maryam and was about my age, spent a while at her brother's who was one of the respected neighbors. Saeed, Morteza, Nader and I had agreed to leave her alone. The first few days, when Maryam with her brown eyes and golden blonde hair in white chador would join the other girls who every evening would sit together at a doorstep and talk, passed. The girls would dust and broom the alley and the boys would play street soccer. Meanwhile, there were eye contacts, with no conversation. A while later, Saeed broke the news and told me that Maryam had fallen in love with me with all her heart. Those kind of love, about which Maryam would talk to the girls, and I would talk to Saeed. Whole summer, there were lovely eye contacts between Maryam and I, with no words. Summer was over, and Maryam left her brother's house. Later on, from the girls of our neighborhood, I'd receive lovely letters with no words, but pictures; like a heart hit by an arrow, or Xs which meant lovely kisses, or a crumpled paper with the letters of "I love you" on its margins. In fact, lovely letters in the 60s (1980s) generally resembled a treasure map. They were nothing more than hints and signs which meant a girl loved a boy. Some of the letters got to my mother because of the writers' unskillfulness. So, one of my mother's daily routines had become looking out the window while I was at school, so that she'd make sure no one would write her son any letters. I, on the other hand, sometimes to show off, would tear the letter in front of my mother or the girl without reading it, whenever I received one. My mother was afraid that the guards would find out about the letters and put me in trouble. I wish the grownups knew that if boys and girls talk to each other normally, there wouldn't be any lovely looks or forbidden relationships. One incident that'd keep lovers of West Aban Alley away from each other, was the effects of war and aerial bombardments and rocketing in Tehran. Every night, for a while, an Iraqi war plane would cross Tehran's sky and fire once or twice. Almost all neighborhoods in Tehran got hit at least once. Even our neighborhood. Every bomb would demolish a house completely and after about an hour it was like there'd never been a house there. A flat desert. After some years bombardment was replaced with rocketing. During the days, usually two or three rockets were fired simultaneously, and would hit a spot in Tehran. I think it's a war strategy that, aerial bombardment takes place at night and rocketing happens during the day. Every rocket would ruin one or some buildings and the houses around them. Wherever the rockets hit, everyone would be killed and some others living in the houses around, would perish of the shattered glasses. Bombs and rockets pushed it so far that people from Tehran went homeless, just like people from Ahvaz, Abadan, khorramshahr, Dezful (western cities exposing the war directly) and etc. At nights of bombardment Tehran would migrate. An inundation of people would set out for the suburbs like Damavand, Roodehen, Khavarshahr and Karaj. Some would take refuge at their relatives' houses and many others would sleep by the streets and highways. The families, when slightly away from Tehran, would spread their sleeping mats next to each other, prepare tea and fruits and dinner, and finally would go to sleep; altogether. And then in the morning, they'd go back to school and work. As the bombardment got more severe and rocketing started, the schools got closed and obligatory migration of people from Tehran got prolonged. My family also, to survive, went to a village between Ghazvin and Hamedan. A village where all the residents had the same family name.

The case of love and lovers in West Aban Alley was closed this way. My father's industrial workshop, where tank parts and bullet cartridges were manufactured one day per week, also got closed. There was a huge difference between what we'd see as war and what they'd try to show us. At school, no day would go by without war ballyhoos. Defense Preparation was the name of a school subject at secondary school. Every once in a while, some people in dusty colored military suits would come to school and fire tear gas and make a scene. They'd make the school

13

students crawl in the yard and would excuse that we had to be prepared for any kind of battle situations. They'd teach us how to dismantle and assemble the Kalashnikov; and also, how to throw a grenade. In my whole education life, I don't remember anyone, from school mates to the kids from our neighborhood and relatives, going to war voluntarily. There were usually trucks around the crowded crossroads and some people drafting others to the war. Whoever who looked around eighteen would be apprehended and dragged to the trucks. They wouldn't even mind the mothers' begging. For years this method of drafting was common and eventually when the war was over it got out of fashion. Back then, though, all the papers hanging on the walls of school, and all the videos of war, which they called The Holly Defense, broadcast on TV, were unlike our observations. On TV and in the interviews, the soldiers were all volunteers, and the martyrs, according to a weekly documentary series called Ravayete Fath (Conquering Narrative), were all saints. In the 60s (1980s), my uncle got arrested for having some books and served a couple of days in Evin prison, he'd played unconscious after a couple of slaps and then they figured that he wasn't member of any political parties and released him. I'd hear about many people, mostly youngsters, getting arrested those days. My mother's cousin, who was a member of the mosque activists, had hidden his books in the air vent some days before he got arrested, therefore, in the Revolutionary Guards' raid on their house no books were found. He, who'd been rejected at the Islamic Republic Army selection interview, went to military service after he got released. They sent him to the war and after a while he got killed, or in other words, martyred. The alley they lived, got the martyr's name. They put a metal cylinder, as big as a car, with hundreds of colorful lightbulbs on it, in their alley for forty days. The government gave them some money. The relatives stayed at their house for seven days, in black. His mother said that the body they'd showed her didn't resemble her son, the guards, though, told her that this is the one who saved a whole troop with his bravery and got martyred himself. Twenty years after the war had finished, one of the martyr's family members said that he'd gone to war as a volunteer. Those days, the other reason to go to military service, which meant war, was this: the high schools would give the boys their diplomas only if they went to the military service right after graduation. It was after ceasefire between Iran and the rest of the world that I saw some people around my age or older going to the front voluntarily. When I asked the reason, they said that if you spent three months and some days at the front, the possibility of getting employed by governmental places would be higher; and also, you could take the advantage of your attendance at the front and go to the universities more easily. After the war had been over, apart from the minefields, there were no danger.

Nader, who knew how to talk with grownups, was a tall boy and was at some age when he'd get taller two centimeters per day. Once, Nader had been detained to be drafted. It took his parents like two days to prove that he was still underage to go to the war, only by declaring his ID. Some days after the incident, Nader would hold a cigarette when walking down the alley and he wouldn't mind the tidy creases of his clothes anymore, and you could see a sorrow in the depths of his eyes. The older boys wouldn't generally go to the military service. They didn't because they were afraid to get killed in a war which wasn't ours and they were count as fugitives. They couldn't either get married, or get a checkbook, or get employed, or continue education, or get the driver's license. Such group of people, who were actually count as unofficial people, were growing more and more every day. In such situations, some youngsters would leave the country illegally. One of the most common ways was that the truck drivers would prepare a space underneath their trucks and put the war fugitive boys there and drive them out of the country. The truck drivers initially figured out this way for their own sons, but after a while transferring the military service fugitive youngsters to other countries, became a lucrative business; as well as building a space underneath the trucks.

Some months after the bombardments had turned into rocketing in Tehran, my father decided to start a business in the village we'd taken refuge. While we were in the village, we settled in two rooms at the corner of a villager's house. It was the only house in the village where there were water faucets, but since there was water in the pipes for only one or two hours a day, we had to get water from the qanat a few stairs under the garden. Washing hands, face, teeth, clothes and dishes would all be done after descending a few stairs down to the qanat by a current of water in which you could also see little goldfish swimming. In winter, the garden and all alleys of the village were full of mud. To go to school, I had to walk several kilometers and go to a classroom with students from first to third grade of secondary school. Long later I learned that such classes were called multigrade classes. The teacher was so excited to have me and another boy from the city and would try to show off our knowledge to the others from the village so that he could create a competition among kids and the villager boys would study harder. The villager nerds were good at course book materials but we, urban kids, were better at solving math problems and general knowledge. The villager kids, anyways, were more prepared for life than urban kids. They knew about their parents' jobs much more than we did. About the field and methods of harvesting, they were more knowledgeable than an agriculture graduate. They knew how to irrigate the field, so the water current wouldn't take away the strawberry bushes. In the middle of the desert, they'd go from one hill to another on their own with no fears.

Getting homeless because of the war wasn't so hard to me. All concerns belonged to my parents. No troubles would be transferred to me. I'd have the feeling I had to grow up overnight and not gradually. Every day my classmates and I would pass by a big garden of almond trees. In springtime, we'd climb the trees which had born green almonds and would pick and eat them until the peels would turn into shells. But the fruits on other trees would never finish. After almonds, it was time for peach and fig peach and nectarine and other tree fruits. Every week, one type of fruit would get ripe and there was a glorious celebration of fragrant juicy and colorful fruits on the way back home from school. When it grew hot enough, we made a glorious discovery. There plenty of swimming pools in the gardens around. Pools mean swimming to the urban kids, but to the villager kids it means irrigating the farms. The water first gets to the pools next to the farms, then the farmers lead it to the fields. Every day in summertime, we'd go to a pool and enjoy the nature and swim. My younger brothers and sister, who were five and four and three years old, also would play around the pool and garden and would pass the best period of their lives. Many days passed by like this. All my father's efforts to open a chicken farm in the village were inconclusive. My father lost everything first during the revolution and second right after there was peace between Iran and Iraq. And the last time he lost his courage to start over. I could see a bitter sorrow in the depths of his eyes.

All the homeless from West Aban Alley went back home after the war finished and I had this feeling that the clock hands were moving faster than before. One day suddenly, everything changed. Kazem came to the street soccer field behind the alley and surprised Saeed and me who were practicing shooting the soccer ball by the left foot. He, whose hair style resembled Bruce Lee's those days, said that he'd beaten one of his coworkers at work. They'd had a fight and the coworker had annoyed him so much that Kazem had torn his face by a chisel, which is a metallic tool looking like a screw driver and is used to carve wood. Saeed and I didn't have a proper understanding of what he was saying. We thought he was lying or worst case, it'd been a simple fight like those we sometimes had with the other kids. Some days later we saw Kazem's coworker at their doorstep. An adolescent boy whose both sides of the face was bandaged up and there were tens of stitches on his cheeks. His family paid a huge fine, so he wouldn't end up in jail. From then on, there was a distance between Kazem and us. His new friends too different from us. Saeed and I also had eventually concluded that Kazem was sometimes insane.

Sadegh's father, two or three years before the war finished, had moved to Tehran from a village, along with the whole family, and had become a guard in Sepah's Revolutionary Guard and by a car, behind which was written 4WD would wander around the city and remained in that position after war finished. His job had become patrolling days and nights and arresting young boys and girls who would walk together, or those who'd rent or sell movies. Sadegh, the oldest son of his family, after changing jobs three or four times, eventually became a thief. First time he, at night, burgled the garage he worked for the excuse of his low pay. Next time was when he worked at a spare parts shop. On the street he'd sell things he'd stolen; one day a West German driller brand of which was Bosch, the other day a gearbox, and the other day rings and pistons from England, and the other day wrenches or screw drivers. The more professional he'd become, the more our relationship would fade. We'd lose whatever we had in common day by day. Nader's father, who'd been one of Shah's bodyguards, had lost all his life after the revolution and had been thrown to a small house in West Aban Alley and every once in a while, would thank god for him and his family not having been executed. Quiet and meek, he'd work at a real-state agency around the corner of East Mehr Alley. He kept doing the same work after war. Nader, after war, became a soldier through his mother's groans. Compulsory military service killed all his motivations and life wishes and day by day, made him gaunter and skinnier.

Morteza's father, who had a dozen of kids, died after years of sickness. His wife, after forty days, got married to another man. Morteza was hardly seen in the alley after his father's death. Mostafa, his younger brother who'd grown up, quitstudying and went to work.

A while later, Kazem got lost. I mean we didn't hear from him for a year, then he showed up and said that he'd been in jail. He'd been charged with burglary from a factory's depot. His accomplice, though, had taken all the responsibility and then he got released. Kazem, after a while disappeared again along with his accomplice's wife who was an adolescent girl.

Sadegh, who'd made a remarkable progress in robbery and thugs and bullies respected him so much, had grown to another level and for the first time introduced us Cannabis. He'd stand by the alley and hold a cigarette and hit its butt on his left thumb nail. Saeed and I were strangers to the things changing rapidly around us. Habib, the placid boy of the neighborhood, also started smoking. Initially, Saeed and I wouldn't let him smoke in front of us, but later, there was no way. A short while later, Habib, who worked at a tailor's, had to go to military service and got separated from us and the neighborhood. I hadn't finished my third year of high school when I got out of adolescence overnight. Before my father got sick, Saeed and I would play street soccer every evening. My days without Saeed would be spent on cycling. But after my father got sick, I grew up overnight. When the final exams were over, because my father had to breathe some air other than Tehran's, we sold our house and left West Aban Alley; to somewhere far away. Another city, neighborhood, alley, where I never made a friend. I got so far away from my past that it took me twenty years to shake the memories. A past lost in the 60s (1980s).

Women are always the source of inspiration. Even, those whom you've talked with only some words. Dena's eager eyes threw me directly to twenty years before. The spark of a bitter sorrow which I saw at the back of her eyes, would indicate her eagerness. As much as I was, to bring back old friends.

A Knuckle-Deep Ocean

We'll probably set out tomorrow or after tomorrow. I have some deferred works to deal with. Today I should fix the air conditioner, so the kids wouldn't get annoyed by the heat while we're not around. I should also tune the satellite antenna. Winds and storms of Ordibehesht (Apr-May) have made it untuned. I should also pack my stuffs. I must pick up two or three novels for the road. Pen and pencil, shaving razor, tooth brush, towel, two sets of shirt and pants, USB flash memory, camera, cellphone, socks, underwear, swimsuit, towel, bag, backpack, bread, ten or twenty canned foods, charger, Ranitidine.

I'm supposed to function as my mother's bodyguard. My presence grants her security. Last time, when she traveled to Istanbul with her friends, she felt unsafe. I was in a fog about her trip. Or she didn't say anything, or if she did, I didn't hear. But this time, when she decided to travel again, she tagged me along. Her purpose is business and mine is being with her. The obscurity that can come in traveling, appeals to me. After a long time, I'm slightly excited to do something other than writing. So much that I've got off the seat in front of my computer and I'm preparing for travel. In a single day I'm both fixing the air conditioner and tuning the satellite antenna. For about two years I haven't done such things. I mean I've done nothing. I've only read and written. Every day in a room, through the window of which you can only see the sky, I sit in my chair and write. Nothing can get me off my chair for too long. The only matter that can take my one or half a day is dating my girlfriends. Girls who have proclaimed they don't want any physical relationship because they want to be with me till the end. I've never understood how these two matters are relevant to each other. These are one of those inseparable things which can be found only in my and Iran's territories, nowhere else. Nature always takes its course. Perhaps while traveling to Turkey I find a new love. I don't know. Perhaps, the conditions in Turkey would turn out in a way that I could stay. Perhaps I could go to Greece through there and then go to Europe and start a new life. But what will happen for my son if I want to stay away from Iran for too long. Until he turns seven, his mother has his custody and every effort to convince my ex-wife to give me my son's custody is destined to fail. I have no interest to talk to her, let alone trying to convince her. During the last years that she was my wife, we'd disagree on 100 percent of the matters, and now that our only connection is our son it goes the same way, there's nothing in common between us. This is why we don't say a word to each other when we forcibly visit every week. We don't even say hi. I say hi to my son in a way that he assumes I've said hi to his mother as well. I haven't even looked at my ex-wife's face for the past two years. I have no interest. I'd like to not see her. It reminds me of years of torture. Or perhaps it's a part of the punishment I've planned for her. The best punishment for the one I once loved is to withhold my passion from her. I have never been able to understand why a spouse and a mother can cooperate with the government against her family. I had no debt to her. The last time that I was protecting her, I did one of the rare work of my life. I lied. All is allowed to protect the family. "I do not love you anymore." After that, I was sure they would not hurt her.

I'd told her that "I have no more passion to you". Passion is verbal relationship and look. I withheld both from her.

My mother has arranged the round tickets on the phone. She's transferred the money, and all she has is two bank receipts. The bus driver's phone number, who's going to set out in Tehran and pick us up in Karaj, has been given to us so we could arrange where and when to expect the bus. The bus is supposed to leave Tehran at 2:00pm and I anticipated that we should be in front of the bus station in Karaj at 2:30. We have two backpacks, one of which, full of bread, canned chicken and fish, some boiled eggs and potatoes, a small saucepan of Dolmas, and a couple of plates and spoons and forks, nestles on my shoulders, and the other one with a towel in it, on my mother's. An empty suitcase, a bag with some books in it, two cellphones, a camera are all we have along with our passports. "Don't bring any clothes other than what you're wearing. We'll buy whatever you want over there." Said my mother walking from room to room. I set out in khaki casual pants and a white and cream striped T-shirt and sky blue sneakers on one side of which is written Love (in English) and on the other side Hate (in English). Setting out for a country I don't have enough information about. My information about Turkey is limited to what I've heard from the news on TV. I know that the Turks have a laic government, a prime minister has been in power for years, in 2006 a Turk writer has won the Nobel Prize and I've only read one of his books called: My Name Is Red. I remember from the school books that Ankara is the capital city and Istanbul is a historical city which in European boarder. On the other hand, I know that there's a play put on the stage about compatibility between Islam and democracy in Turkey and the last time I saw Turkish national soccer team playing in the World Cup gloriously and made their people proud. I do not know enough about the people's culture and customs, geography and history. My only object of delight is the book of "Turkish for Travel" which I bought years ago but never read it. Turkey is accused of the Armenians' genocide, and on the other hand they don't have a good relationship with the Kurds living there.

At 3:00 pm, we'll get on a golden bus with single seats on one side and double seats on the other. There's a narrow carpet spread in the aisle, which is why the one who sold us the tickets said that the bus is called VIP. We sit in our seats number 7 and 8. A young woman who's sitting ahead of us next to her husband and is playing with his arm hair, slips her fingers among her husband's fingers, puts a heart-shaped pillow between the two seats and gets her face close to her husband's face, but the young husband is either indifferent or trying to convince his wife to sit quietly. After his avoiding every time, she draws her headscarf forward a little. Ahead of them, Asal a thin girl, who looks ten with golden hair reaching her waist, is sitting next to her grandmother who's a woman with puffed up face and bulky lips, and when she wants to look around she has to turn around; Asal, occasionally walks in the aisle and talks to her mother who's a beautiful woman with half-covered high-lighted hair and sitting in a single seat.

Half an hour after we pass Zanjan, I've reviewed Turkish alphabet a couple of times and have learned that "Gunaydin" means good morning,

"Evet" means yes, "Tuvalet nerdedir" means where's bathroom. I've also finished three chapters of Orhan Pamuk's book My Name Is Red. There's a nonsense movie playing on the two screens installed at the front and in the middle of the bus, which I wonder why the director, writer and actors have wasted their time making such movie. As far as I understand, the story is about two young hobos who both are wearing Indian clothes and pretend to be rich, so they can scam others. A cheap copy of Bollywood with a happy ending. Bollywood people wouldn't make such a wishy-washy movie even three decades ago.

In the 60s (1980s), when Iran was at war with Iraq, the time when there were only two TV channels in Iran and VCR was considered a forbidden contraband, Iran was overflowed with Bollywood movies. Those days there were every type of movies in Iran, but Indian and Turkish ones were the most popular. Those days people would see every movie in which Ibrahim Tatlises had a role; maybe even more than the Turks themselves. In the absence of European and American movies, a generation of Iranians were sorely moved by Indian and Turkish movies. Turkish and Indian romances made up for the absence of love in a country where any kind of earthly love was forbidden.

On the right side of the road, the sun is showing off amongst the clouds, on a blue road sign it's written: Fasten Your Seatbelts. On the left side of the road, it's full of dark clouds. Asal, who so far I've figured is going to forth grade this year, is dancing in the middle of the bus with a bit of charm. She'd enchant me if I were twenty years younger or she were twenty years older.

We can hear a singer from the speakers:

-look where eventually it went, the story of me with you... (a Persian song)

It has rained here, it rains here, it rains much harder here. Asal laughs out. I hear the singer from the speakers above me:

-if you're determined to go, sorry if I couldn't change your mind... (a Persian song)

******

At 3:30am, at the Turkish border, there are hundreds of cars and buses waiting in parallel lines. I guess we'll stall here for some hours. Carrying the suitcase with my backpack on my back, I get in the Customs along with my mother and the other passengers. I find out that we have to pay the bank ten thousand Tomans each, as exit tolls. Everyone speaks Azari at the counter. I don't understand anything they say. Iranian Azari people are known to be chauvinists. I think they overdo it. I've been to Tabriz a couple of times and once they knew that I didn't know Azari, they wouldn't even answer me. Long time ago I faced the same situation in the town of Miyane (near to Tabriz). I'd ask people for directions in Persian and they all would answer me in Azari. This characteristic isn't epidemic though. As much as the people from Tabriz and Miyane try hard to keep their distance from the others, people from Orumiye are hospitable and unprejudiced.

The line to the exit tolls paying in the bank is getting smaller quickly. But it stops occasionally. The bus drivers have to pay a fine for gasoline; out of turns.

Gasoline is cheaper in Iran than it is in Turkey. Even, two years ago the prices of gas and gasoline went up first 100% then 400% and then 700%, and then got rationed, still oil products are cheaper in Iran than they are in Turkey. This is why taking substances like gas and gasoline from Iran to Turkey is so beneficial. Some bus drivers take gasoline up to one tank, which has the capacity of 300 to 400 liters, some others have a hidden tank and take more. Some cross the border carrying barrels of gasoline and gas. The government's excuse for raising the price of gas was the very same thing. To convince the public opinion, it was announced that due to the low price of fuel in Iran, huge amount of fuel crosses the borders. Therefore, the solution is to raise the price inside the country!

Iranians wondered why should Turks and Afghans buy our fuel so cheap and sell it so expensive! Thus the price of gas in recent years (for Iranian citizens) went up from 70 Tomans to 700 Tomans per liter. One person wants to pay the exit tolls for all the other passengers. Some try to get themselves to the head of the line out of turns. But as I figured, paying in or out of turns makes no difference. Because to move on, all the passengers have to be done with paying before crossing the border.

We should also pay Red Crescent Society one thousand Tomans. Totally eleven thousand Tomans per person. I show the officer sitting in a small room, my passport and the bank receipt. A man with four stars on his shoulder. He has stubbles. He lacks hair on the front of his head and speaks Azari and I don't understand a word. I also give the major my mother's passport with the bank receipts. He stamps the passports. Seal of exit Iran. Unlike my expectations, no one searches my suitcase and backpack. My mother says that the Syria passengers have crowded this place. She means there are many people who want to travel to Syria. The women who want to go to Syria are recognized in their spotted chadors. Bunches of men and women who want to go to Syria are sitting in the chairs in the hall of the Customs building. Women in headscarves and spotted chadors and men in pants and with stubble on their faces.

Another officer controls the passports in a small cabin. He looks me in the eye closely while he's paging my passport. If he's skillful enough, he can recognize a bitter sorrow at the back of my eyes. He scans my passport. I'm a little anxious.

During the trip I asked myself for a couple of times, what if they arrest me? I didn't have any reason for this delusion. They will be happy if I leave the country and never come back. I think the main reason for this anxiety is that in Iran all of us are count as criminals somehow. The way we dress, our satellite antennas on the rooftops, the playing cards in our closets, blogging without the government's consent, taking a walk with a girlfriend on the street, they are all forbidden according to the law, shariat, and traditions. Especially now that we're close to Khordad 22nd (June 9th). Outside of the Customs building, there's a vast area, a part of which is covered by gable roof. Under the half-open ceiling there are two carpets with red background, spread on the ground. Syria travelers are sitting on the carpets. On one carpet there were men with stubble and pants and shirts, on the other women with scarves and spotted chadors. Out of the gable roof area some are sleeping on small rugs. Some others are leaning against each other shoving their hands in their jeans' pockets. It's five in the morning and looking at the line of the cars, it's clear that we have long time to go. Maybe we have to wait for another hour. I spread a rug and put flask of tea on it. My mother prefers to stay inside the Customs building where it's warmer. I eat some. A boiled egg and a potato. I offer some people tea. A bit away from me, there two people sitting on a rug. One of them calls my name. I get shocked. I don't know how he knows me. Maybe we've met before. Maybe his child was my student before. But I don't think so. He clearly wants to connect. He's one of those whom I call warm-blooded. He asks me to wake him and his companies up when the bus arrives. I say:

— alright. I'm awake.

I lie down and put half of the rug on me. I put my head on the suitcase. I tie my hand to the backpack. I've gotten goose bumps, my bones have frozen, I've curled up. I fall asleep at 6:00am. I wake up at 7:00.

I look around a bit. The two guys are still sleeping. All under one blanket. Someone in jeans approaches me.

— you'll catch cold. Get on the carpets.

He says.

I say no it's fine. But immediately I figure I've said bullshit. I'm surprised that someone is paying attention to me. For years, I have only seen attacks and threat and insults and lies about my self. Syria travelers have left. There are some people sitting or sleeping on the carpets. I put my stuffs together and get on the carpets. I cover myself with the rug. I tie my hand to the backpack. I put my head on the suitcase. "Why ever did I trust my mother and didn't take anything warm?" I ask myself. I get warmed up a bit. I get my head out. I can see a beam of sunshine over the hill next to the watchtower where Iranian flag, some meters away from Turkish flag, has surrendered itself to the wind.

There are new Syria travelers sitting around me. Women are in headscarves and spotted chadors. There are also a couple of men lying down next to me. They've come from Kashmar. One of them is a girl about thirty, and the rest are over fifty years old. The girl isn't wearing a ring and unlike all other women is wearing a white chador. She looks around with her eyes. Murmuring quietly, the women mind their own business. "There are still three buses ahead of us" says my mother. Some of my fellow travelers have gathered at the exit door and are chatting. I sit; with my mother next to me. "We've been waiting here since 3:30am last night." I tell Syria travelers. They answer:

29

— we've been here since 2:30.

The sun is up. I'm still cold. We're sitting under a tall gable roof between two hills, one of which is Turkish soil and the other is Iranian. My mother's wearing two sets of clothes; one suitable for Iran and the other good for Turkey. I'm bored. I'm tired; of waiting. It'd be better if I knew how long we were supposed to wait. Those two, whom I were to wake, are up. Together, we decide to cross the border and wait for the bus on Turkish soil. Others join too. We pass the entrance gate to Turkey. There's a long line at the cabin where an officer's sitting and stamping the passports and allowing people to pass. There's constantly a fight over the turns. Everyone after passing this cabin, have to wait for their companies, many of whom are still on the other side of the border.

The Turk officer argues with someone. Gets out of the cabin, slams the door and leave. It takes 15 minuets for another officer to replace him. He gets in the other cabin. The line falls apart. Those from the tail of the line goes to the head of the new line. The fights get intense. It takes half an hour. I hand over my passport to the young and good-looking Turk officer. He pages it. He glances at me. He stamps in red. I enter Turkey. The sky is blue everywhere.

Iranians are sitting on the ground in groups. The talk to each other. Talking to them or even hearing them bores me. I get separated. I spread the rug close to them and sit. My mother chats with others. I hear someone saying:

— god is light, he's energy, god is inside you, god is you.

— just say there's no god and free yourself!

The argument's gotten intense. I get separated. Recently Iranians have been dealing with self-examination and theism crisis. I myself have the same problem. I've been looking for myself and God since the age of fifteen or sixteen. But I don't think I can find God among the Passengers' talks at the Turkish border. I might find myself during this trip, but god cannot be discovered at the Turkish border. Has anyone found the meaning of God in the whole history.

According to the Old Testament, he is a wrestler. According to the New Testament, he is light. According to the Quran, he orders the massacre of non-Muslims. How many religions are there in the world?

The bus experiences the roads of Turkey at 3:30 in the afternoon. The first sign to show off is Mount Ararat. The two peaks, slightly away from each other, make a glorious prospect. A young man says that the remains of Noah's Ark has been found on one of the skirts. I've also read something similar on a website. But there was no evidence. There were some pictures and a hypothesis that this is Noah's Ark fossils. The only thing I know about archeology is that you can estimate the age of an object by examining the isotopes of carbon. Isotopes are atoms of one substance with same amount of protons and different amount neutrons. The ratio of isotopes of C12, C13 and C14 are stable. Once a living creature dies, its C14 start deteriorating. It takes 5700 years until it becomes half. So, if a fossil object has 25% of normal amount of C14, it means that it has the age of two times of 5700 years. There was nothing about the antiquity determination written on the website. Anyone can claim that they're standing on Noah's Ark fossils right now; or even on the Salomon's Carpet. Was a ship built in the world thousands of years ago and all the animals were riding it? How many animals?

Around the road, the hills are so green. The houses which we see on the roadside, have gable roofs. The walls are mostly yellow and red. I see harmony between the nature the Turks' constructions. No construction disappoints.

There's a minaret in the middle of a small gathering of houses. The mosques follow the style of the Muslims' prophet and have one minaret. In the beginning of Sultan Mehmet the forth's kingdom, there was an Arab sheikh called Sheikh Ostovani, who had murdered someone in Damascus and fled to Turkey and there he finds some disciples. He prospers so well that many appointments are put to action following his opinion. This hypocrite and corrupted sheikh, who'd sell job positions to the highest offer, considered building mosques with more than one minaret against the prophet's traditions and haram. Many years later, during the early days of Mehmet Koprulu being minister, Ostovani's disciples gather in Sultan Mehmet Mosque. They agree to destroy all tekyehs, and make all dervishes convert to Islam, and murder those who resist, and ban using gold or silver dishes and silk clothes and tobacco. Some theologians get armed with sticks and knives and along with some merchants gather in Sultan Mehmet Mosque and threaten the dervishes by howling and shouting. Koprulu first tries to calm them down by sending some representatives, but since they don't care about his demands, he gets the Sultan to execute or exile the heads of the revolt.

Some kilometers after Erzurum, to rest, the bus stops at a place with gas station and shops and restaurants and a playground for children, for forty minutes. Karami says that this big recreational complex has initially been a small store whose owner has been trading gasoline from Iranian bus and truck drivers and this is how he's become rich and even once he's become a member of the parliament.

There's going to be an election in Turkey next Sunday. In front of the restaurant, there are thirty or forty cars, on the hood of every one of which they've put a red flag which is the symbol of MHP "Nationalist Movement Party". Youngsters are wearing a white cap on which it's written "SES VER TÜRKIYE". One of them holds his pointer and baby fingers towards me. The other one gives his white cap to my mother. He laughs. I hold my pointer and baby fingers towards him.

The bus starts moving. I hear from the speakers above me: Recently a girl has become my heart's playmate... (a Persian song). I've read another three chapters of Orhan Pamuk's novel. I've learned from "Turkish for Travel" that Ne Kadar means how much/many, Ekmek means bread, Bir means one, Iki means two and Uc means three. My bones squeak after two days of sitting and two nights of sleeping while sitting. The last stop is a restaurant near to Istanbul. As usual you can find everything from A to Z at the shop next to the restaurant. I empty the flask and then fill it up with hot water. I pay two Liras for the hot water. There's also canes, wooden swords, toys, cradles, trays, earrings, shoes, slippers, cookies, and even a book stand. I take a look. All books are in Turkish. I see "Snow" and "Istanbul: Memories and the City", by Orhan Pamuk. These two novels haven't been translated in Iran. Price: 20 Liras. I pick another book. Karami says that on the book it's written fifth publishing 15000 copies. Karami shows me a book. On the footage there's vague picture of five Ottoman sultans. He says that the Ottomans ruled five times, a hundred years each. Ottoman land was so vast that its territory would spread up to the city of Vienna, it included a big part southern Mediterranean sea and Arabian Peninsula, from north it was restricted to the Don River and from east to the Persian borders. Ottoman Empire emerged in Anatolia in 13th and 14th centuries, they considered themselves as the heir to Islamic Caliphate since the turn of 16th century. During a significant part of Ottoman history, apart from the Sultan, all princes were excluded from government positions and resourceful and competent men were the heads of affairs. The right to have four official wives didn't include the Sultan. Sultan's wife would be chosen not from the well-known and credible families but from the handmaidens since their childhood. Thus, the wife of the Sultan of the time and the mother of the next Sultan had no relatives to interfere with the governmental affairs.

We arrive in Istanbul at 9:00am. The highway, where we float in the traffic, reminds me of highways in Tehran. The Turks go to work and it seems to me that citizens of Istanbul are so calm while driving. Everything is calm. No one is in rush. Perhaps I shouldn't jump into general results based on little observations. I look at the brands of the cars passing our bus. Renault, Audi, Toyota, Peugeot. I don't recognize some of them. Maybe they're produced in Turkey.

The bus stops at a travel agency. I get off. On the windows of the travel agency it's written in Persian: Tehran, Tabriz, Isfahan, Shiraz. Once I get off someone gives me a flyer. One-night ferry tour, Arabic dance, Sama dance. $30 per night. Karami points at a bridge down the street where we're standing, saying that I can find him and Ali and his company at the first hotel on the first street after the bridge. We shake hands and get separated.

Carrying the suitcase with the backpack on my back, my mother and I go looking for a hotel. At the first hotel, a two-bed room costs $40. Same room at the second hotel is $50 and the third $60. We visit some other hotels as well. The prices are $50 or $60. My mother says that they rented an apartment the other time and it was cheaper. On some papers on the windows of some stores, it's written: rental apartment. The prices range from $60 to $90. I learn that my mother and her friends, in her previous trip, rented an apartment for $60. They were six women, so $10 each. I just realize the reason why rental apartment is cheaper. We go back to the first hotel. There's a grumpy boy instead of the good looking woman we saw first, chatting online. With fingers I show him that we're two. He calls his mother. The woman I saw first walks down the stairs. She has a smile on her face. She nods and her son, who looks fifteen or sixteen, gives me a key, on which it's written 303. I get the luggage. The boy and his mother say somethings that I don't understand. The woman put two fingers together and then separate them. I again don't understand. I feel. I say (in English):

— She's my mother.

I throw myself on the bed. "How enjoyable lying down is" I say. My mother laughs. I fall asleep. I wake up by the noise my mother makes. The clock on the wall says it's 11:00 o'clock. It's 12:30 on my cellphone. I've been sleeping for an hour. I'm still ready to drop and the wrinkles on my belly and stomach haven't been ironed out yet. "Let's go to the Friday Market" my mother says." Everyone's going the Friday Market to shop." I nag a bit. But I give in eventually. My mother leads me: "we should go this way". We go. As we keep going I feel like she doesn't know where we're headed. "Do you know where the Friday Market is?" I ask my mother. "This way" she says. My feelings tell me that as always, in her life she only wants to go, and it does not matter to her that she is in the right direction or not. Of course, this feature in Iran is an epidemic. I stop her. "Let's see where we're going."

I ask someone (in English):

— can you speak English?

He squints, pushes his finger on the bridge of his glasses and points with hand (in English):

— Aksaray

— ok

— left hand

— ok

— 2 hundred meters

— thank you

I figure we should go back to the way we came. We arrive at the bridge.

I ask someone (in English):

— do you know Aksaray?

He points to the ground with his finger. We turn left. We run into Asal and her companies on the stairs to the Friday Market entrance. Asal is standing among them in pink shorts and T-shirt and a white cap, holding a Barbie doll. Her uncle glances at me. We give no sign of knowing each other.

The Friday Market is a collection of some vertical and horizontal allies. Narrow or wide. The sellers are standing on the sides of the allies. They've laid down their stuffs on the tables and are shouting. "On Leira On Leira On Leira Pantolon." Since they shout in Turkish I don't understand them. The traffic made by the buyers is heavier than the traffic in highways of Istanbul and Tehran.

The women grab the clothes one by one, take a look, and then the next clothe get dragged out from among a hundred of other clothes. I ask the prices. "Write down the prices" my mother says. I take notes in my mind. Men's T-shirt 10 Liras. Women's slippers 5 Liras. Jeans 7 Liras. I learn the prices. Most of the products in the Friday Market cost 3, 5, 10 or 15 Liras. Hardly can you find 40-Lira-women's shoes or 20-Lira-jeans.

A little girl, around Asal's age, stands in front of me. She has black eyes and eyebrows and dark hair. She holds, the bottle of water she's holding, towards me. Her eyes sparkle. She says something I don't understand. I read in her eyes:

— it's hot, and you're not carrying a bottle of water, and I sell water. So buy one.

I take some coins out of my pocket. I put them in the palm of my hand. She picks one. Half a Lira or in other words 50 Kurush.

We get out of the Friday Market at 5:00 pm according to Turkey's time. We Stoll. I don't look at the stores. I mostly notice the way people dress. Unlike my country, men and women here have no limitations on the way they dress. It's been eighteen years since the quality or style of clothes didn't matter to me like today.

Eighteen years ago, when I was a student collage, in my first working experience at the age of eighteen, I used to work for a wear production company as an errand boy. I would do bank works or deliver the goods to the retailers or do the shoppings. After a while the boss rented a store. It was around the corner of Valiasr street and Jomhuri street. Where they call Jomhuri crossroad. After a short while I learned about different types of cloths such as crepe, silk, linen and cotton. I also got familiar with the styles such as English collar, night gown, crew neck, middy and etc. After some months when there was a customer, I'd choose what I wanted to sell before they started talking. I'd make a connection between their face, skin color and age, and there was no way that a customer leaves a store, where I was the salesman, empty-handed; unless they didn't have money, in which case, they would come back some days later and buy my recommendations. After a while, thanks to Kamran who'd been a salesman for many years, I learned to set the shop windows. Kamran was a forty seven-year-old man, almost bald, except for a line of hair on the back of his head, and had a wide mustache. He had a beautiful wife and two little boys who'd go to school. He'd worked as a salesman for many years and in many parts of Tehran, and in clothing business he was an expert. I learned everything about clothing business from him while we were colleagues. The most important point was that I had to speak with every customer in their own language; polite with the polite, street talk with the thugs. I had also learned the salesmen's language:

— dafo ro becher chonimeh. It means they're good customers, treat them well.

— zighast. It means they're just window shopping and won't buy now.

I wouldn't look at the women in chadors in the eye. I'd keep a physical distance. I'd chat with more modern girls and women and would drown in their eyes, and would sympathize with those men who were desperately looking for some clothes which their wives would like. This was how I made regular customers. The religious women were glad to have found a salesman, dealing with whom they'd feel safe, and they would bring their friends along to the shop. The girls were satisfied with me drowning in their eyes and having only a friendly conversation with me while shopping, and would call on once or twice a month to shop for new clothes. Those who'd sell themselves to a salesman at the storage in return for a manteau or a raincoat, were astonished by my double behavior.

While I'd respect them as humans, I wouldn't care about the type of deal they had to offer. I got plenty of job offers from the shops around with a couple of times more salary during the six months I worked there. Simultaneously, my boss asked me to marry his daughter. The marriage proposal thing had me think more seriously. For the first time, I thought about being a clothing businessman for the rest of my life. The thought of companionship with some thugs, who smoked opium for fun, would repel me. I knew I'd get carried away even if I were saint. Anything or anyone wouldn't appeal to me in the market so that I'd remain in that business. I couldn't remain in the shop after refusing the marriage proposal. I quit clothing business for good.

Two tall women with sunburnt skin are packing a handful of clothes in front of the elevator at the hotel. I lay down our shoppings between the two beds and toss myself on the bed. I wake up with the noise of the door opening. My mother say:

— the shower's not hot. The woman says half an hour later.

I take a cold shower. "Cheap is cheap" I say while showering. We take a walk in one of Istanbul's streets at 8:00 pm. There are advertisements for different brands on the walls of the high rise buildings. I look at the shops one by one. There's a tramway passing through the middle of the street. I notice the names of the streets. Yashiltulumba, Laleli, Ahmetpasha. I memorize the way back. We reach a park. I don't know its name. It's a big park. Some noise attracts our attention. Around the corner, some young people are performing a play on a large stage. "I wish Atash was here" I tell my mother.

Atash is an actor and a member of an art group in Iran. Such opportunity to put on a play in the park is a dream to him and his friends. To perform a play, they have to get the script approved by the government. Then they have to rat race to find a place to put the play on. There are many stages for theater in the parks in Tehran, but they're usually not used. Around a hundred of people are sitting on the benches near to the stage. We sit. There are two men and two women from Eastern Asia sitting ahead of us. On our right, there are some people, whose face look like people from Eastern Europe. Some people speak Persian occasionally.

We walk down the park. We reach a big mosque. It's become dark. "Let's take a look inside the mosque" my mother says. According to the brochure my mother got at the entrance of the mosque, I figure that we are in a neighborhood called:

Sultan Ahmet Cami. According to the guide sign at the entrance of the mosque I figured that women without hijab and men in shorts can't enter. The same laws that exist in Iran regarding men's shorts and women's hair are also held in a mosque in Turkey. We put our shoes in a plastic bag and hand them over to a safe keeping place for shoes at the entrance. My mother wears a blue headscarf which is given to women and then we get in the mosque. A glorious architecture, peacefulness and a line of the prayers and visitors, number of whom goes up and down constantly. I get mesmerized by the greatness and peacefulness of the mosque. I'd like to sit here for an hour and sink in my own. In the mosque there is a positive flow of energy. I feel it.

It's become cold outside. My bones are freezing again under the T-shirt I've been wearing since the beginning of the trip. "Let's go back by tramway" my mother says. At the tramway station I figure that we have to get chips. I search and find a chips vending machine. I don't understand the writings and signs on the machine. The red or green buttons don't ring a bell. A man, who has a painters woolen hat and is sitting in wheelchair and has a slight smile on his face, speaks to me in different languages. He guides me (in English):

— 3 Liras

— red

— green

— ok

I grab the two chips out of the machine. I buy a pack of tissues for one Lira to say thank you, from the Indian or maybe Iranian man. He's one of those who put bread on their table by sitting next to the vending machine and guiding the tourists. I look in his kind and free of expectations eyes. I say (in English):

— thank you.

I think the man in the wheelchair is so much at peace. Why haven't I been at such peace? Maybe he was pretending. Maybe that apparent peacefulness has to do with attracting the tourists' attention and eventually his daily income. He probably has chosen his job, but I cannot go to a job that I am interested in because of the interference of the security forces.

The tramway is crowded. Just like the subway in Tehran around this time. There's a blue line indicating the tramway route and the name of each station at the top of the door.

Yusufpasa, Aksaray, Laleli, Beyazit, cemberlitas, Sultan Ahmet...

"Let's have Turkish food tonight " says my mother. We get in a restaurant. I look at the menu. It's all in Turkish. I see the word "Doner" among the words and pictures. "Doner" I tell the smiling waiter. By my fingers I show him two portions. I calculate, 10 Liras each portion, plus beverages, we should probably pay 25 Liras.

"Do you have any plans to continue living?" My mother says. "Not yet?" I say. "Can you stay in Turkey?" She says. "I do not know Turkish. How to live without my son?" I say. "Do not worry, he will grow, and, in the future, he will understand everything." She says. "They have taken everything from me; my wife, my friends, my job, my credit, my home, I do not let them take my son again. I will resist to change the circumstances. In other hand, they control my ex-wife. That's why my child's place is not safe. So far, if they have not damaged him, it's because I have been lying that I do not want my baby. And they have believed. There is no other option mom, I have to wait."

The waiter serves the food. On every plate there are some meat, some rice, some cumin, some mashed potato and a meatball resembling a grenade. The meet doesn't agree with me. But I'm hungry. I've lost so much energy in the las thirty hours. My mother only eats the rice and the mashed potato. We pay 33 Liras and get out of the restaurant.

I drop on the bed. Till the next morning.

*****

It's a couple of minutes to 7. A young boy, on whose white T-shirt it's written "SEX" in bold, is preparing breakfast in the lobby. I wave at him to say hi. He nods. The breakfast includes boiled egg, some salami, some olives, cheese, butter and jam. The young boy tells me to grab a tray through some gestures. "My mother's sleeping, I am waitin for her" I say. I don't know whether or not he gets me. I sit on a cream colored sofa in the lobby. I read one more chapter. A man talks to me in Turkish. "I don't know Turkish" I tell him. He says "Bashar Asad, Mobarak, Ahmadinejad". I assume he's either sympathizing with Iranians whom he's seen on TV getting beaten on the street or he's asking for news from Iran. "Ahmadinejad is nobody" I say. I don't whether he gets me. How to say that in Iran, according to the law the president is nobody. I feel jealous. He takes pity on me -an Iranian-.

Two years ago, on Khordad 22nd 1388 (June 12th, 2009), there was a play on stage in Iran called presidential elections. The "intellectuals" had convinced people to vote. People hoped that their votes would make a difference. The intellectuals were certain that people's votes wouldn't even be read. The day after the election, people came out to the streets, some of them carrying a banner, on which they had written "where's my vote?" Three days later, on Khordad 25 (June 15), three million people - as estimated- took part in the Rally of Silence in Tehran. They were holding banners:

— where's my vote?

From that day on, thousands got imprisoned, an unknown number of people got killed, and many had to immigrate illegally, in other words, escape. And many security forces were transferred abroad to form a fake opposition outside Iran. It shook the earth. The left-wing, in all countries, wore green wristbands and rallied on the streets to support the Iranians. The scene where Neda -a girl from Tehran- was dying on the street, got broadcast all around the world. Months of conflicts between people and soldiers in Tehran woke everyone in the Middle East.

I don't know whether I'm like someone whose vote has been stolen, or someone upstanding who's fighting for freedom, or an idiot whom the intellectuals of the world are trying to convince to change, otherwise all bullets will be triggered towards me. My mother sits next to me with a breakfast tray. I get a breakfast tray and two cups of tea from the young boy. I eat my egg and cheese and olive. My mother eats only cheese and olive and tea. Other guests at the hotel arrive one by one or in groups. Three or four women are sitting at a table in front of me. They look like Armenians. I don't understand a word of their language. Package shows that all of these women have traveled to Turkey for business. "Today we should go to the Saturday Market" I tell my mother. "Is there any Saturday Market?" she asks with astonishment. "I don't know" I say, "there might be". "We should go to Martah" says my mother. "Martah?" I repeat. "It's the capital of jeans" she nods. By asking people, I find out that to go to Martah we need to take the subway. I put three Liras in the machine and get a chip for two people. I look at the top of the door in the carriage. I read the names of the stations. I learn where we should go isn't called Martah. The correct name in Merter. A neighborhood packed with clothes shops. Clothes for men, women and kids; bags, shoes and of course jeans. My mother buys whatever she wants or doesn't. I buy a pair of jeans. I wear them right there. There is almost no more jeans without chafed or torn spots. But eventually I find one. I lose my sunglasses forever, where I buy the jeans. I learn today that clothes measurements in Turkey differ from those in Iran. They go like this:

10/32 12/34 14/36 16/38 18/40

Same numbers in Iranian and European style are like:

36 48 40 42 44

This is why, to buy someone a pair jeans, the best way is to have their every measurements in centimeters. We arrive at the hotel and I prefer to have my tuna can, which I bought in Iran, with the Ekmek (Turkish bread) which I bought here for 1.75 Liras. So does my mother. I lie down on the bed. My mother goes out to get herself lost among the sales.

I wake up. I haven't been recovered from the journey. My mother has showered and is drying her hair. "The water is hot" she says. I go to the bathroom. I wait but the water doesn't warm up. I take a cold shower. "Paying $10 less per night isn't worth taking a cold shower" I think.

My mother says:

— Let's go out and see what's going on.

Although I don't feel like going out, I go with her. She goes to one of the sales. I sit down on a vase up the alley. I can hear an Iranian music from speakers at the sales. A young man with shaved head is standing by the wall up the alley. "Iranian?" He asks. I nod. He says:

— interested in prostitutes?

— no

— Iranian, Turk, Russian and Arab girls. Let's go I'll show you.

— how much?

— how many hours?
— Three hours.
— it'll be thirty Liras.

I calculate that with the income of thirty Liras a day you can't even afford a hotel room. "Shall we?" He asks. "No, some other time" I say. He stares at me. I go to an internet cafe and sit down in front of a monitor. The keyboard layout in here is a bit different from those in Iran. I have a hard time finding @. In Iran I would press Shift+2 to type @, but here Shift+A doesn't type anything. I ask the person next to me for help. Alt+A is the one I'm looking for. After some failed attempts to reach my email I figure that there are two keys for the letter "I". I finally get to check my emails. I take a look at my weblog. There number of visitors to my weblog has been varying from 700 to 800 for the past few days. My latest book, which I'd published online and underground, has been downloaded for 1700 times. The internet spread in Turkey is wonderful compared to Iran. You don't have to wait for any website to open. There's also no need for anti-filter or VPN. Facebook is wondering why I'm logging in from another country. I have to answer some security questions. It shows me pictures of my friends and I have to choose the right names. With this much obsessive security, I wonder how my previous Facebook account got hacked last months. Three months ago, I found out that I couldn't login to my personal Yahoo and Facebook account. The hacker had replaced my Facebook photos with some pictures of dead bodies from Auschwitz. They'd also posted some edited pictures, on which there were some watchwords against the current rulers of Iran. Some say that "Anonymous Soldiers of Imam Zaman" are to blame. In Iran, those who work for the Iranian secret service (Ettelaat) are called "Anonymous Soldiers of Imam Zaman". Imam Zaman is the twelfth imam of the Shiites who's believed to have divinely disappeared and would return on the judgement day and would introduce the real Messiah. No one knows for sure whether such a person really existed at all. Historical surveys show that the Twelfth Imam has never been born from any mother.

I've heard that they've hacked emails that are so active. The only result for me and them was their access to some of my novels before publishing. Some say that those against the Islamic Republic are to blame. Nowadays, as always in the history, you cannot tell the difference between right and wrong in the news. It smells like burnt frying oil in the internet cafe. It bothers my chest. I can't breathe anymore. My throat is dried and burns. This respiratory disease is also a prison repository. I pay two Liras and leave the cafe. My eyes are welling up with tears. I feel like I've caught cold. Runny nose has added to my bone-ache. I go to the hotel. I lie down on the bed in the room 303. I use two blankets so that I will sweat. At midnight, I wake up with nausea. My mother gets worried. "I just need to rest to get well" I say. The next morning I wake up for breakfast. It's 9:00 am. My mother's just woken up. After breakfast, my mother gets separated to go shopping. I sit in the lobby. I grab the remote control and change the channels. I have hard time finding Persian channels. I hear that Ezzatollah Sahabi, the leader of the National Party in Iran has passed away. At the funeral, his daughter, Haleh, who'd just been released from the prison, has also passed away. They use the verb "pass away" on all channels. There have been many news like this since Khordad 22, 1388 (June 12, 2009). I have a feeling that those who are capable of being organized political activists die more regularly than the others these days. The truth behind any news is usually revealed years later. It seems, The right flow in Iran is emerging and the left is dying.

There's a man in white and red and purple striped shirt having breakfast at the next table. "Are you from Iran?" He asks. I look at him listlessly. "I've just arrived" I say. He says that he's been out of Iran for business eight years. I say that he's done right.

Economy in Iran is dead. Everyone has to kind of scam the others till these days and years pass. The sanctions have paralyzed the government and also the people. People, however, have been paralyzed for years now. "What's your job?" He asks. "I'm a teacher. I was." I say. He laughs. "I don't work for the government." I say. "How come?" He asks. "there are two types of pedagogy in Iran. One governmental and the other private. I never became governmental."

I say:

— Do you know what "selection" is?

— It means choosing.

— In Iran, selection means an official inquisition. Those who want to work for the government, have to pass this test with honors. I find it offensive. This is one of the reasons why I didn't become governmental. "There's been chaos in Syria too. Bashar Asad is killing people in Syria. Any news from Ahmadinejad?" He asks. "In Iran, the president is nobody. He is the president of nothing. I say that the word "republic" has different meanings in every country in the Middle East. The Iranian government appears to be a republic. But in truth it is a kingdom. The first person is not the president but the leader. Also, in Syria. The Republic of Syria is not a republic; It is a dictatorship. Elections in these countries are just a ridiculous show. Votes are never counted." I say. "Everything's destroyed in Iran. It's not fixable." He says. My mother sits down next to me. She cues me not to talk.

The man lights up a cigarette and I cough. I'd started smoking since 18 years before. Once I had an argument with my roommate and then I got out, bought a cigarette and lit it up. I became a smoker since then. I smoked Winston for a while. Then taking a friend's advice, who said those were fake, I went for Montana. Two years later its taste changed. Montana was said to have become fake too. Then I went for Downhill green. Until recently which I changed to Kent 7. During the years, I decided to quit smoking a couple of times. Once I bought a pack of pistachios and didn't smoke for a day. But before the pistachios finished I started smoking again. I had three more failed attempts, but didn't work. Whatever it was I enjoyed smoking it. This was exactly why I couldn't quit. It looks silly. Until recently, like a year ago, my throat would swell and I couldn't breathe when I smoked each time. Prison has destroyed part of my health forever. I had to reduce the amount. The coughs kept on for some months. Eventually I'd get out of breath after the first puff. I liked smoking so much. Cigarette and I looked inseparable. But I couldn't smoke anymore. I did every thing but I couldn't. It's been six months since the last cigarette. The coughs also stopped after I quit smoking. "Don't sit next to the smoke" my mother says. "Your chest isn't fine yet." The man puts out his cigarette and leaves.

With my mother, we have lunch and spend the afternoon on a pier by Marmaris sea; next to some fishermen and tens of different boats. We agree to go to Taksim after some rest. I've heard that it's tourist area. But I have no idea what to expect. On the way back from the pier, we go to the travel agency. "We've paid for the tickets back in Iran." I say. The young man says:

— it's none of our business. There's no empty seats for tomorrow.

"Whose business is it?" I ask. "Call where you paid." He says. "It's an official holiday in Iran now." I say. He says:

— it's none of our business.

Today in Iran, it's Khordad 15 (June 5). In 1342 (1963) which is 48 years ago, there was big rally on the street against Mohammad Reza Shah's kingdom in Tehran. Some got killed. The rally was held by the religious. My father's friend, who was twenty then, got shot. My father says that there'd been some dead bodies, shot on the streets, in the hospital, where his friend had been kept.

My father says that it was then, when he'd first heard of Khomeyni.

17 years later the Shah's kingdom gets dismantled and the religious kids, led by the clergymen come to power. Shah was the one, some of whose work was completed by the revolutionaries thirty years after his death; assigning the factory shares to the workers. The revolutionaries, who were supposedly fighting for freedom initially, when came to power, annihilated the one freedom which formed late at the end of Shah's kingdom: freedom of speech. Khomeyni, the leader of the revolution, who became the Supreme Leader of Iran, name of which had turned to Islamic Republic, died eleven years later on Khordad 14, 1368 (June 4, 1989) in a hospital in Tehran. Khordad 14 and 15 (June 4 and 5) have been announced legal holiday on Islamic Republic calendar.

I talk with my brother on the phone. I tell him what happened at the travel agency and ask him to follow up with our tickets so that tomorrow we can get on the bus which goes back to Iran. We get out of the hotel at 5:00 pm. I know that under the Aksaray bridge there's a road sign written on it: Taksim. There are some taxi vans after the bridge. There are small signs behind the taxi windows saying:

Aksaray — Taksim.

"Taksim" I tell the driver pushing my thumb and pointing finger against each other. He makes me understand that it's two Liras per person. After passing a neighborhood, where Black Sea and Marmaris Sea join, we arrive at the great Taksim square. Tens of green collared pigeons are pecking at the ground among humans. A woman and a man and a child are selling cups of wheats among pigeons and humans. The tourists scatter the wheats on the ground. This is how the man, woman and the child with cups of wheat and the pigeons put food on their table.

Around the corner, there are some men and women standing in a row and chanting. In front of them, on the ground, there are pictures of some men and women. And there's a flower on each picture. I can't understand anything. On the biggest banner on the ground, it's written (in Turkish):

PIR SULTANLAR OLMEZ
GONDOREN PIR SULTAN ABDAL
DERNEGI
I ask some people (in English):

— What's the matter?
I find a woman who knows English. I say:
— I'm from Iran.
"Are you a Shia?" She asks me.
I want to say that my religion is not how I am recognized through. I guess it must matter to her so much. I nod. While putting together her black hair from the back to tie. "The Sunnis have torched the hotel where the Shias were staying. 18 years ago." She says. My mind stops working. Being Shia or Sunni becomes a matter of life and death to me. I thank the woman. Religion is the only excuse to hurt others.

I look at the statues placed at the hight of three or four meters in the middle of the square. A lot of people are coming and going. We turn onto a street name of which I can't find. There are so many people there. Both sides of the street are packed with clothes shops. Corns and acorns and mussels are also very popular. Every now and then the tramway passes through the middle of the street. Thousands of people are taking their Sunday evening walk. Some youngsters have put a table on the side of the street and according to the music and the red flag with a yellow hammer on its middle I guess they're advertising the Turkish Communism Party TKP. There is no party in Iran. Islam is a way of managing a country that does not need parties. The only Iranian government tool is baton, tear gas, bomb, and a bullet. Making every day the organized lies should also be added.

I lose my mother in the crowd. It takes half an hour till I find her. She's still window shopping at every shop she sees. We grab a Doner wrap at night. This time chicken, 2.50 Liras each. I find it tasty this time. We call on the travel agency. A middle-aged lady tells us politely that they had a phone call from Tehran and our tickets are ok for tomorrow at 2:00. I run into Reza and Karami outside of the agency. Karami says that their bus sets out for Iran tomorrow at 2:00.

Tomorrow is our last day in Istanbul. The next morning, I go to the Internet cafe to enjoy the privilege of high speed internet and my mother goes to the clothes shops around the hotel. She shows me the suitcase and backpacks she's placed next to the reception desk when I get back. She's checked out. I put the backpack on my shoulder and drag the suitcase to the travel agency. We put them under the waiting seats and get out. My mother is looking for some shops she hasn't found yet. In the last moment, when we're getting on a van to go to the bus terminals, a vendor sells three full sets of women's underwear to my mother.

We wait in the Istanbul sun for half an hour for the other passengers who are coming by the next van. It takes nearly one hour to load everything which are supposed to be taken to Iran from Turkey. The driver asks for extra money for every extra suitcase. A couple of passengers complain. The bus departs. Reza and Karami are sitting ahead of us.

We're all glad to have good companions during the trip. I read two more chapters of the novel. My mother pours tea and Reza offers dates. Karami turns back towards me and asks:

— how much did you pay for the T-shirt you're wearing if may I ask?
— 10 Liras.
— last night I saw three of them for 10 Liras under Aksaray bridge.
My mother asks excitedly:
— where?

— right under the bridge.

My mother says:

— we were out last night, what time was it?

— 10 to12.

Karami brings forward the sleeve of the T-shirt he's wearing and says:

— I'm afraid mine is of a better quality than yours.

My mother says:

— I wish you'd told us too.

— I didn't know where your hotel was.

I laugh inside. "We finished our money on the first day in Istanbul. Mr. Reza spent all our money at the first shop. Last night we realized that we didn't have any money left to check out and for the road. We put a hundred of the T-shirts we'd bought on sale under Aksaray bridge. Each three for ten Liras." He says.

I fall asleep around 11 at night and don't wake up till 7 in the morning. Karami is sleeping under the seats and Reza on the seats. My mother and I in our seats. The bus stops at the same recreational station on the way to Istanbul. We have bread and cheese and tea as breakfast. We have one or two hours until we reach the border. The youngsters who are sitting at the front, start dancing to the music being heard from the speakers above. Two young women, one of whom looks 30 and the other looks a bit older, start dancing with two young men. The others clap. The two young women make other youngsters dance too. There's a line of dancers in the aisle. Unlike me, everyone is so talented at dancing together. The two young women are even better. The type of the music from the speakers above changes every couple of minutes and so do the dances. They put on an Azari music. Karami gets up. He puts one hand on his back and dances with his feet. They put on a Kurdish music. Around ten people stand next to each other, make a ring with their pinky fingers and start bending forth and back. One of them grabs my mother's scarf and spins it in the air.

We reach the border. Everyone has to get their things and get off the bus. There are only some buses and some cars behind the gate. Once I get off someone who's standing next to the bus tells me that I can buy his suitcase right for 35 thousand Tomans. "What does it mean?" I ask. "Everyone can only have 20 kilograms of luggage when crossing the border, if you have extra you have to pay a fine. Those who have extra luggage will give them to those who don't have any to carry for them, per 20 kilograms cost 35 thousand Tomans." My mother explains. The Customs officer doesn't let Karami cross his luggage. He says that he has too much luggage for one person. Karami says that he can empty half of it. The officer looks at him in awe. Karami looks at me desperately. The officer searches my suitcase. He says that this is too much for one person. I say that we're two. He says that I can't cross this much luggage. I ask if a person can cross 20 kilograms... he says no, 7 kilograms per person. I look around. There's no board with the rules written on it anywhere. My mother drags the suitcase herself. Around the officer there many people like Karami who are begging for crossing permission. My mother goes ahead with a suitcase and a backpack. I follow her. The officer turns a blind eye. They don't search our backpacks. We could have crossed a gun, bullets or at least some beers with 5% alcohol. Karami also slips away. Lack of law, or perhaps lack of willingness to execute the law ends up to our advantage for a short while. At the same time, more than a hundred packs are coming out of the building. All of them are the name and address of one person. In my opinion, however, these many clothes crossing the border paralyzes the Iranian producers. The modern textile machines can't get imported into Iran due to the sanctions. Iranian textiles are of low quality. Iranian producers have to either produce low quality products or import textiles from other countries. We haven't reached self-sufficiency in this matter yet, just like the other matters, after 32 years. I think we won't get independent even after 320 years. Getting independent seems like reaching the core of the sun. Customs fees on textiles is so high by the excuse of domestic production. Producing clothes by imported textiles costs so high in Iran. Turkish clothes are both of a better quality and cheaper. I conclude that fighting trafficking in my country is more like a cultural action and is not practical at border. Or maybe no sane person would smuggle drugs or weapons from Turkey to Iran. I should actually be glad that they didn't take my fingerprints or take off my clothes to search. We sit down among Syria travelers whose number is more than Turkey travelers outside of the Customs building. A group of Syria travelers including men and women are sitting on the ground and having lunch. Rice and Ghorme Sabzi (an Iranian food). Women are in dark spotted chadors and men are in pants. An old man who look 70 years old sits next to me holding a toothpick. He asks:

— back from Turkey?

— yes.

— is there any holy shrines in Turkey?

— there are lots of mosques. Even more than in Iran. When it's Azan time, you can hear it from everywhere in the city of Istanbul.

Syria travelers have been waiting to cross the Turkish border for about 11 hours. We've been waiting for our bus to cross the border for 4 hours. The bus crosses the border and a few minutes later stops at a restaurant for lunch. The desire to have an Iranian dish is recognizable in the line of people. Most of the orders are koobide kabab and chicken kabab. I do what others do. I grab a tray and two spoons and forks. Soup is on the house. We eat a plate of Iranian rice with two sticks of koobide kabab. This is the only and most favorite food to all Iranians and my mother. We take a walk. The walls are covered with graffiti: "we'll stand till the end".

I wonder what "end" means? The biggest difference between this side and other side of the border is the covering of the buildings. Iranians like to use marble in outer walls of the buildings. But in Turkey the walls are mostly painted in red and yellow. On this side you can see the pictures of the previous and current supreme leader everywhere. At the Customs, restaurant and on the walls around the city.

On the bus, I talk with Karami and my mother with Reza. Karami tells me the story of his life; My wife and I had a clothes shop in Bushehr. We'd been married for like two years. My father in law took his sons to Mashhad. He also tried to convince me to go with them. His reason was that I was a good tradesman in a half a million-populated city; so I could boom in a two million-populated one. I sold my shop and became partners with my father in law and his sons. I moved my whole life to Mashhad. Some months later the Islamic Republic accepted the Resolution 598. After that the trades slackened. I would do whatever I wanted until Mashhad, but there I had to convince three others and then inform my father in law about anything that had to be done. I was totally weakened. After some months I said I'm out. My brothers in law had put

250 thousand Tomans each, and I'd put 500. Two times more than each. When I gave up, the Resolution had just been signed. "The business is slow you know." Said my father in law. "And there's no money. Come and get 20 thousand per month." I had no choice. I'd lost everything. I was totally broke. I rented a photography studio around the Shrine. It took me a year to put myself together again. The quality of my photos was unique in Mashhad. However, after a while the quality of my photos degraded. I couldn't find the reason. Back then we had to stabilize the films. There were some containers with some chemical solutions in them. We had to put the films in them in order. First container, second and third. Other than that, it'd destroy the films. We had to renew the chemical solutions once a year. I would change them once a month, but the quality deteriorated every day. I eventually got tired. I did whatever I could and didn't have any idea anymore. I gave up the studio. Two years later I found out what was going on. The owner had a cousin who'd been supposed to rent the shop before me. I didn't have a clue. After I rented the shop the cousin could still go there. Man, every day he would replace the solutions from one container to another; only to destroy my business and make me leave. I moved to Tehran after that. It'd been a few days since Saddam had attacked Kuwait. The Americans had also attacked Iraq. People from Iraq had refuged around the Iranian borders. I went to the Ministry of Foreign Affairs and inquired. I said that I was a freelance photographer and intended to go to the borders. They said that some foreign reporters had happened to be there and were going to the borders. They'd formed a sort of organization for this. There was a guy named Heydari whom I asked to send me to the borders along with the foreign reporters. He looked at the guy next to him and said:

— alright. The reporters fly tomorrow morning at 7. You can join them by being at the airport at 6. I flew to Urmiya the next morning. Then we went to Piranshahr. We reached a point where there were barbed wires between us and Iraqis. Only a sedan could fit through the space they'd left on the road and there were a couple of Iranian officers with guns standing and letting nobody passes through. It got suddenly so crowded when the reporters arrived. They all spoke different languages. Some of them crossed the border and the officers took them back. I crossed the border in that chaos. There were two or three rows of cars up to 75 kilometers long. The farther I got the more disastrous it became. People had to get away from their cars to pee. They would go to the desert. I didn't have a clue that there were mine fields around the road, and so many dead bodies. Children were crying. People said they'd had no food for three days; they didn't have water. I was just taking photos. An American reporter who had crossed the border like me in that chaos, was taking photos some meters ahead of me. We were glad to see each other doing the same thing. I finished my films. I told the American: "Let's go back, I have no more films." He gave some so we wouldn't go back. "Let's go farther." He said. We walked ten kilometers until we finished all the films.

Some days later, back in Tehran, I went to the Foreign Affaires Ministry again. I met three Japanese reports who didn't know how to go to the borders. I talked to them in English. They agreed to pay $100 a day if I took them to the borders. I talked with the same Mr. Heydari, arranged everything and went to the borders again. $300 was a good money back then. We came back to Tehran after three days. The first thing I did was to call my wife and tell her to pack our stuffs come to Tehran. Then I rented a house.

One day I went to Ferdowsi street. I went to a photography studio. I said:

— I'm a photographer. I was in Mashhad and have come to Tehran recently. I'm looking for a job. The owner looked at me and told me to go ahead and develop those films. Back then, the color films had a blue or red backlight, and making the backlight disappear while developing the films was the best of a photographer. I did it better than the owner himself. So he said:

— come to work since tomorrow.

I worked there like for two months. There was no digital cameras back then. There were film reels. Kodak, Fuji... The photographers would dump the reels after using them. Once I took the used reels home and bought some chains on the way. Then at home I put them together and made keychains. Every day after work, I'd go behind the municipality and vend the keychains to people at the shopping mall. It was good. Per day I was earning as much as I would at the studio in a month. So I quit the studio. I rented a basement in Fardis turned it into a keychain workshop. I'd buy all of the used reels from the studios in Tehran or other cities. The keychains were packed in 12 and sold to all markets in Iran. After a while, I could buy a house through this job. A year later the competitors grew more, so much that it wasn't worth working anymore. At the same time I had met someone who sold movies in Tehran. Animated movies on VHS. Those days personal computers were new trend. I thought I could copy the movies on CDs and sell. I bought two copies of each movie. They became about 70 I guess. I also bought a PC. It took me three months to install a CD writer on my PC. I asked everyone how to do it for three months, but no one seemed to know. It took me another three months to find out that I could install more than one CD writer. I installed three more of them. It took me three more months to find a software that arranged the CD writers to work in turns. Then I started to copy the animated movies. Gradually we developed CD boxes made of printed cardboard.

I myself learned to work with Photoshop and designed the boxes. My work prospered again. Initially we'd sell the CDs in the market. Then developed it. We gave the CDs to the supermarkets. At first the salesmen didn't agree to sell my CDs. I'd leave some packs and tell them to give me a call if they sold them. In less than a week they'd call and ask for more. It worked perfectly and I became the king of animated movies in Iran. They knew me in this name in the market. King of animated movies. I bought a shop through this job. I had half of the money and borrowed the other half. A while later my friend, from whom I had borrowed money, went bankrupt. The current government had just taken office. To save him, I had to sell the shop and pay him back. When I sold the shop the page turned. It was rumored in the market that I went bankrupt. Until a week before that I could buy everything on my credibility but after I sold the shop they wouldn't even give me a box of raw CDs. I figured it wasn't gonna work. I sold my house to buy a shop. In the meantime the price of property went up 4 times. I mean the shop I'd sold for 40 million Tomans, went up to 160 million Tomans in three months. The house I'd sold for 20 million Tomans went up to 80 million Tomans overnight. For the first time in my life, I held my hands up to surrender.

I printed cardboards for the covers of the CDs which cost around 75 million Tomans. I also had raw CDs which cost around 10 million Tomans. I copied movies on the CDs. But the market was slow. A business downturn. I mean because of the sanctions, the best supermarkets in Tehran, to which I'd give a thousand CDs per week, couldn't sell even a hundred in a week.

How much do you think I sold the printed cardboards?

— I didn't know

— make a guess

— you probably had to pay!

— I sold them to those who turn paper into dough for 90 thousand Tomans. I paid 30 thousand to the workers to move them to the truck.

That's how I got broke again. It was the time when both of my children were about to go to university. Of course I'm doing my best to pay for their university at the moment. Only I don't have an appropriate professional look.

I moved to Fardis from Tehran since I lost everything two years ago. My rent in Tehran was 260 thousand Tomans. In Fardis I rented a place for 60 thousand Tomans. I talked to someone in the municipality and asked them to give me a spot on the street so I could sell my CDs. I was vending CDs. I wouldn't disturb anyone. The municipality gave me a spot on the sidewalk and I would do my job. Someone else sinned somewhere else but, I paid the price. Members of the municipality had a fight with some vendors in the streets. The vendors killed one of them. Thus, the State Ministry sent a circular letter to all municipalities in all cities banning vending in the streets. This is why I couldn't keep on working in Fardis either. Now in Karaj, I'm working in front of Mr. Reza's shop. Until I find a way to start over. This was my life story. You can turn it into a novel.

Ups and downs in Karami's life have made me put my hand under my chin and drown in his words. My mother and Reza are talking enthusiastically. She says:

— human cannot fall in love with god, because they can't understand him. In fact, god falls in love with human; If you want more information, you can go to underground mystic classes.

A couple of people are lying down in the aisle. Others in their seats. Tabriz is behind us. I think we'll arrive in Karaj 6 or 7 hours later. Karami speaks Azari with the one who's sitting ahead of him. I recline my seat to sleep. Asleep, I fall.

I've curled up in my seat when Karami wakes me. We're close to Karaj. It's 4 in the morning in Iran. My mother and I, along with Ali and Karami get off the bus next to Fardis bridge. The bus leaves for Tehran.

*****

I sleep for some hours. I regain the energy I've lost. At lunch, my mother says that Reza was surprised by our relation. He said that his mother had stopped talking to him for a year. She's told her son that she wouldn't have any relation with him unless he throws out the liquor bottles and starts praying. He was welling up with tears while saying that. "Religious work is to separate people from each other." I say.

I call Atash. "I'll come to you." he says.

I have a chat with Atash. He reads 2 or 3 chapters of the novel I've eventually finished after years. Golchehreh. "Is the audience of the book only high school students?" he says. "No, the main character of the story is a high school student." I say. He says:

— I'm tired. We have a performance tomorrow. You should come too.

I copy the novel on CD and give it to him.

*****

I travel 70 kilometers by bus and subway to get to Khavaran Culture Central. This place, which was built around 20 years ago, has put together the kids in the neighborhood, who would formerly become criminals or junkies, and has transformed the area into a cultural center.

Karbaschi, the mayor during whose time this cultural center and many other similar places were built in Tehran, got arrested in 70s (1990s) and along with all his colleagues got imprisoned for years and got deprived of all services and activities.

Atash has the role of a homeless old man on a bench in the park. The social atmosphere has nothing to do with the plays they choose to put on. I've told Atash many times. But every time I've been answered: we must.

The regime is harassing dissidents. There are hundreds of organized government-related crimes, every day. Newspapers across the country are just lying. The opposition abroad does nothing but to deceive public opinion and deceive the governments and politicians of the world. The opposition groups are more pro-regime than opposed to it. In this situation, watching a theater, which is the only entertainment aspect, is a waste of time. It's like you screen the movie The Message on September 11 in the United States; or like you put on the movie Not Without my Daughter, at the opening of the festival of friendship of Iran and the USA; or like you invite Condoleezza Rice or Saddam's daughter to the opening of the conference of Violence Free Movements.

"There are two problems. A person who authorizes theater performances and reads texts does not have any understanding of literature and art. You imagine that a sheep is responsible for this. I am the next problem; I do not want to go back to jail again. You know, I'm not worried about myself. If I'm arrested again, my mother will stroke. I do not want to see again that my mother begs the interrogator and the judge to not execute me. I have no problem with execution. But I am not willing to ask the Islamic regime."

*****

I get my son from his mother at the same night. He should stay with me for the following week as his mother and I agreed after more than two years that I did not know where them were.

A while ago my ex-wife contacted me after two years or so. "You do not want to see your son." she said. "No." I said. "He is sick. You must see him." she said. I guess it might be a fresh trick. "I have forgotten that I had a child." I said. "His kindergarten teacher said that this child should see her father." From the tremor of her voice, I recognized that the subject of the illness was serious. I guessed that the kindergarten teacher had achieved some of the truth. So, she tries in her own way, Put them under pressure. "I will see him. When?" I said. "Tomorrow" she said. In any case, that was the situation I had been waiting for two years.

My mother gets him to put on the T-shirt and the yellow shorts she's bought him. My favorite yellow color goes with my son well. I get out of home the next day. I review in my mind the incomplete address that Reza and Karami have given me. Shohadaa square, Beheshti street.

Karami said that if I find Reza, I'll see him too. I go through the whole street once. I look closely at the window shops. I don't find them.

I go back through the same way. I see Reza behind a window down the street. I look around me on the sidewalk. There's no sign of Karami. I enter the shop. There's a customer there. We greet each other. I sit in the chair. Reza sells two pairs of jeans and a T-shirt. "What's up?" He asks. "I missed you." I say. "I came to see you and Karami." "He's given me a call last night when my phone was turned off." He says. "I hate ringing phones." I say. "You've said." He says. "Where's Karami?" I ask. "He comes to work like chairman." He replies. Under the glass on the table, there's a picture of a little boy. He said during the travel that he missed his son. Next customer enters the shop. Reza nods smiling. And then the next customer enters. "What do you do?" he asks. "I write." I answer. "What else?" He asks. "I write." I reply. "What you write won't be allowed to be published." He says. "Eventually they will one day." I say. "I've started a new story since yesterday and for the first time I know its name before writing it." "What is it?" He asks. "A Knuckle-Deep Ocean." I answer. "What is it about?" He asks. "The hero is Karami. He says he's a knuckle-deep ocean." I say. Half an hour passes. Karami enters the shop. We shake hands. He grabs a plastic roll from the corner. He wears a green winter shirt on his red T-shirt and leaves the buttons open. I get out of the shop. Karami has spread the plastic roll, which has pictures of the CDs on it, on the ground on the sidewalk. The first customer is a baby girl who's holding her mother's hand. She picks out one of the animated movies. Karami takes out a CD from a pocket on his winter shirt. The woman pays a thousand Tomans. Karami shows me the pocket he's patched on his winter shirt; four pockets, two on each side. "All of the CDs are here and are alphabetized. This way, if the municipality seizes my stuffs, I won't lose much." He says. The next customer is a girl in chador who asks for a movie called The Secret. She says that she's read the book before and now wants to watch the movie. I guess the customers are regulars. They know Karami.

suddenly Karami grabs all his stuffs and hides in Reza's shop. The girl who's still fumbling in her purse takes a look around. I don't feel any danger. Karami comes out of the shop. "The guy in brown shirt is one of them. He'll get my everything if I don't move it." He says. The girl pays a thousand Tomans. "Although other agents consider my past and future and even my age, and don't bother me, when it comes to survival struggle, their own benefits become more important than mine." He says. "What's extension?" I ask. Adding to one's hair." He replies. "I have a CD about extension which you cannot find anywhere else." "I've started a new story." I say. He says that he's offered some publishing houses to translate Turkish books to Persian but they haven't accepted. Karami grabs his stuffs again and jumps to the shop. There's no sign of a man in brown shirt. I look around a couple of times. He comes back out and points out a car. "That was a municipality car." He says. The sun in the middle of the sky reminds me that it's noon. I get separated from Reza and Karami. I go back home. My son is watching Bee Movie on the couch. I call Atash. I say:

— What's up?

He says:

— if this novel of yours gets published now, you'll have to run away from the earth and live on another planet.

I say:

— you mean I should wait till after the author's death.

He says:

— I don't know. I need to think.

I say:

— we have to say what we have to say.

He says:

— it'll cost you too much.

I say:

— I don't want my son to ask me why I didn't say anything, 30 years later.

He says:

— you should be conservative.

I say:

— I don't know. Let's see what happens.

I turn on my PC. I review my notes on my travel. I start writing the next page.

Awakening

I go to the corporation where I've bought the tickets. I ask:

— When will we set out?

"The bus is on the way here, it's been stuck in traffic, it'll be here in a quarter." Says a skinny man with a curved body.

I say:

— You said the same thing a quarter ago.

He says:

— I gave them a call. They said they're coming.

I take a walk on the round platform inside the bus station. There are names of the cities written on a paper or cloth hanged on the glasses of each corporation. The fares to each city are specified on the boards. I sit in a chair next to Sara. Moving her eyes and eyebrows she points out the old woman sitting next to me. She says she travels alone. She lives here but her daughter lives in *Hamedan*. The old woman leaves her little suitcase with me looking for bathroom. My mother enters along with Ramtin. He has an ice cream in his hand is laughing. "It's 9." My mother says. "Let's cancel the trip if there's no bus."

I enter the corporation where I've bought the tickets. It's crowded. The passengers whose bus is delayed complain. A girl with a cream headband under her black headscarf is sitting in front of a PC and tries to ignore the voices. The curved man is talking on the phone. "What do we do? When will it arrive?" Shouts one of the passengers. "My man think of something. I've been calling them since 8 in the morning and they're not answering. The people have gathered here. I don't know what to tell them anymore." Says the man on the phone.

I get out of the office. The old woman is looking for me and her suitcase in the aisles holding her hands on her hips. I take her with me. And show her the seat and her suitcase. "God bless you." She says. I smile. I take the tickets from Sara. "Where are you going?" She asks. "To the manager." I leave a huge cylinder filled with traveling corporations and find the management office around the corner. I see some familiar words next to the entrance:

"Respect the Customer".

I enter the boss's room. A man in black shirt and pants is sitting behind the desk holding rosary beads in his hand. "Sorry to bother you." I say. "Yes please." He says. "Our tickets are for 8 in the morning, now it's a quarter after 9 and there's no bus yet. I think there's a problem that they cannot solve." I say. "Which corporation?" He asks. "I don't know." I say. "May I see your tickets?" He gets up. He pushes his toes down in his slippers while walking. He gives me a paper to fill out … Client's complaints. He talks with someone on the phone. Once I sign the paper he says: "I talked to them. You'll get another bus." He opens the door and points out a man outside. "He's the manager of the corporation where you bought the tickets."

A man with thick beard, holding a cellphone smiles at me: "I'm so sorry. The bus will be here in 15 minuets." he says. "Are you sure?" I say. "Please wait a little more. We're so sorry. Wait a bit longer." He says. As far as I know the outline "Respect the Customer" is one of the few things in Iran which cannot be bargained. Once a customer brings some charges against governmental or semi-governmental organizations, the guilty party gets punished immediately. This time though there are multiple problems. I think the management has a problem. The bus driver is an irresponsible person. Others are not answering and taking no action to solve the problem.

We get on the bus after 2 hours delay. Some flies are buzzing around. There are breadcrumbs on the floor. And some salt on the seat. Someone is sitting in my seat. I wait until I find a place. All seats get taken. I stand next to the seats number 17/18 and 19/20. Ramtin stands up in the seat and looks back. "Sir, let me empty you a seat." Says the conductor, who apparently knows that I've filled out the "Respect the Customer's form. He gets the two people sitting Ramtin and Sara. "Here please." He tells me. I sit down. Those two get taken to the back of the bus.

I open a poetry book by *Fereydoon Moshiri* and start reading:

Tonight, I won't sleep till the dawn
All my thoughts are for tomorrow
My being is overflowed with pleading for you
The time is asleep and awake in the bed of the night
Weather calm, night dark and road of sky is open
My vision flies as wild pigeons

There's a movie one the screens of the bus. A woman leaves her husband. The man, afterwards, finds some lines of prayer underneath the rug. And also, inside her books. Some prayers for increasing the affection between the woman and the man. Some kids are moving around in the aisles. I recall a period of my life when I had the same destiny as that man. There were lots of prayers inside my books ... I want my husband to be in my control entirely. I read a poem:

The moon, like a girl in love,
Has lain on the sky's laps
Her eyes are busy with glowing
There's a star fall in the night sky
It's like being away from the sun
Is hurting the moon at midnight?
Oh my! She's trapped by love too, just like me!

I feel the bus is swirling. I bend my neck and look at the white line on the road. It turns right and then left. I turn back and look at the passengers, all are sleeping. I close my book and go to the driver. I slip my hand gently on his shoulder. He opens his eyes. "Want some tea?" I ask. "I have here." He answers. What was the deal with the two-hour delay?" I say. "Stuck in traffic." He says: "it's too crowded these days. *Ramadan* is over and everyone is traveling." The bus passes a truck. The driver isn't entirely awake yet. A car swerves around. He says: "he sees me passing, yet increases the speed."
"Shall I pour some tea?" "No, I will"
He tilts the flask of tea over the cup. Now I'm certain he's awake. I get back to my seat. I read a poem:

Oh my heart! Although in this life

You don't wear colorful clothes in happiness
Or you don't drink colorful wine
Or there's no candy on your table
Or your goblet isn't full of the supposed wine
...
If you don't hit the glass of sorrows to a rock
Its seven colors become seventy

The bus stops. I smell rotten fruits, stale sandwiches, and sludge once I get off. I enter a restaurant where apparently only the bathrooms are usable. Is it the bad economy conditions or the dirty restaurant, I'm not sure, but no one orders nothing. I can't find a soap outside of the bathroom. A boy kid is sitting in front of the entrance and asks for 100 *Tomans.*

"You get the money, at least clean up, put there some soap." He moves his head. I feel like there's no will to be clean or to do cleaning. I feel like the life has stopped and the living are trying to pass their lifetime. I tell myself that we're all good.

*****

In *Mashhad*, the bus station has a modern look. It's clean. "Are you going to the Shrine sir?" Asks a young man. "No." "Shall I take you to your hotel?" "No."

We get in Mr.Ali's car outside the bus station. A middle aged man with little gray hair. "Welcome." He says. "How's *Mashhad*?" My mother asks excited. "Nothing much." He shifts the gear. "We last came here two years ago." She says. "It's getting more and more crowded." He points at the streets. "15 years ego they were all farming fields. Now everyone is building four-stories." "*Mashhad* is a big city as a country." I say. His one hand is on the steering wheel and with the other, he points to outside:

— this is *Koohsangi*, have you been there yet?

"I've been there years ago." I say.

While I'm climbing the stairs to Ali's house I meet Ms. Setareh, his wife and my mother's cosine, then Rodabeh who will get married in the following days, then Hesam, Raheleh and Rafoneh.

I stir the cherry juice. Hesam tidies his hair with his hand and says: "I have thirteen units to pass until I graduate as a civil engineer." "You've already done your military service, so you can continue your education as graduate student." I say. "According to our professors, master degree is the same as bachelor." "Maybe they don't want too many students, how come they can be the same?" "I don't know." He says.

"I like psychology." Raheleh looks at me with that sparkle in her eyes. "My ranking is twelve thousand, do you think I'll get accepted?" "It depends on your course selection." I say. There's a movie about mutants hired by the CIA on one the satellite TV channels. There's a war between the good and the evil. As usual, the good defeats the evil. I lie down on the bed in Hesam's room. There's a fish tank next to the bed. The biggest fish is the size of a palm of my hand. It has big fins. It's like a white fish is wearing a black lace. Its eyes are protruding. The smallest fish is the size of a knuckle. Two thirds of its body is green and one third is red. The colors red and green, underneath a translucent layer of its skin is so attractive. Seven or eight small fish are floating steadily and starting at their surroundings. The others are prowling. Their lips are moving. They occasionally dive towards the sands and rocks at bottom and move them. Inside the fish tank, there's a small clay pot, some plastic palm trees, and some big and small seashells on the rocks covering the bottom of the tank. There are bubbles coming out of two big rocks. There's painting hanging on the wall above the fish tank. A boat on a beach by the sea. A part of the sky and the sea and the boat are in dark green. The ground has turned ochre exposing the sunset. The seagulls are flying around a lighthouse. The unusual colors have given the painting a special display. The painter's defamiliarization has made looking at a cliché pleasant to me. There's another painting, which is actually a printed poster with blue background, hanging on the wall on the other side of the room. A child on a mother's knees among the clouds. Apart from two books with the titles Static and Strength of Materials, I cannot see any signs of a civil engineer in the room. I go to bed next to Ramtin. He turns twice during the night. He slips down the bed twice. After midnight he asks for water, "very cold, with ice in it".

Babak Esmaeily

On the breakfast table, there are cheese and butter, homemade cherry jam, date sap, and Olivier salad and tea. "Help yourselves please." Says *Bibi*, *Ali*'s mother. "It's not much. Go ahead please." "Certainly ma'am." I say. Raheleh is wearing a tight collar black blouse under her white and blue chador. She chops the bread on the counter in the kitchen. I wrap a bite for Ramtin. "I want both cheese and butter." Says Ramtin. "With lemon juice. Lots of it."

Around the table, everyone is talking about how people from *Mashhad* would give you directions. "Once asked someone for auntie's home direction, the good man hopped on his bike took us there." My mother says. "I'd do the same when I was single." Says *Ali*. "People from *Isfahan* are bad at this though." Says my mother. "Once in Isfahan I asked for an address, all given directions were wrong." "In *Tehran* people are more interesting. It's hard for them to say I don't know. They get embarrassed if they don't know. That's why when you ask someone for directions, and if they don't know it, they just point towards some direction. When you ask the next one they point at other direction. You rarely find someone who says I don't know." I say.

Reading the subtitled news I learn that some people have been arrested during the protests about the *Orumiye* Lake getting dried.

"Today is *Rodabeh*'s day." Hesam says. *Rodabeh* laughs. "How do you feel about your elder daughter leaving today Mr. *Ali*?" I ask.

"She's with me no matter where she goes, even to Yemen." He says.

The bride's mother leaves the breakfast half finished, and disappears. "Where did auntie go?" I ask. "Setareh still has some tailing to do. She hasn't finished it yet." My mother says. The girls clean up the breakfast table. "You didn't eat any." Granny tells me. "I've had enough ma'am. Always weddings." I say.

*****

The wedding party is held in a garden out of the city. Women's entrance is separated from men's. Everyone is in one garden, just separated with a wall. There's music playing from two huge speakers. There are five rows of eight round tables with five seats around each. The dishes of fruits and sweets are covered in plastic wrap. The wind is gently shaking the edges of tablecloths. The moon is glowing in the middle of the clear sky. I get treated with an ice cream full of cream and pistachio. The groom starts dancing in a cream suit and brown shirt. His father also dances with him. He gives the groom some bank notes while dancing. The bride's father starts dancing too. He gives the groom some bank notes too. The others, one by one, join the dance and give the groom some bank notes. The men's dance in wedding party profoundly involves moving hands non-harmonically in the air and skipping from one foot to the other and shaking their bellies.

I meet the bride's grandfather, my mother's aunt's husband. For the first time in my life I speak with him. I heard he is an important guy in the Revolutionary Guards. "What do you do?" he asks. "I'm a teacher, I was. I write books." I say. "What do you write?" "Poems, stories." "Is there any money in it?" he says. "I mostly rely on teaching, if I can. In Iran they don't give publishing permit to good books." I say. "A book must have a social subject. It should be suitable for both children and adults so everyone can read it." he says. "I've written some books so far but it's not possible to publish them at the moment." I say. "Why?" "One reason is that they don't give me publishing permit." I say. "You must have written something political?" he says. "It's something social." I say. "You're making a mistake. Make money some other how. It doesn't matter how to make money. You can sell beans." he says.

All the novel *The Unbearable Lightness of Being* by Milan Kundera crosses my mind. "I'm waiting for the social and political conditions to get better." I say. "You are unaware." he says. "Why?" I say with smile. "You get yourself in trouble. You'll go down. Your son will also get hurt."

I don't understand whether he's threatening or sympathizing. "I should not go to this trip." I say to myself. "You are making a mistake." he says. Almost all high-level security people use this when they are talking: you're making mistakes. For them Using this sentence is a common way to excel in conversations. Everyone is the same.

The wedding dinner is rice garnished with saffron and one stick of kabab *Koobide* plus rolled beef for everyone. Ramtin is coming and going from men's side to the women's along with other kids. He has dinner at women's side.

Hassan, one of my mother's cosines' son, sits down next to me. "What do you teach?" he asks. "Math." I answer. "Math teachers are all hard as nail." he says. "I've combined Math with love." I say. "Is it true that immortality has gone up in Tehran?" he says. "What does immortality mean?" I say. "It means women go out with their bare heads." he says. "This fifteen-year-old boy was brainwashed." ˉI say to myself. "People of Iran don't like immortality because the concept of family matters to them. What grade are you at?" I ask. "This year I'll become a second-grade math student." he answers. "What would you like to study at the university?" "Process engineering." he says. "You love it?" I say. "No, just because of money. You write books?" he asks. "Sometimes." I answer. "Have you ever published anything." "A couple of them." "What are the names?" he says. "You read books?" I say. "Not me but my brother reads *Rumi* a lot." he says. "Do you read poems?" I ask. "You write poems too?" he asks. "Sometimes." I answer. "People in Tehran are still protesting?" he asks. "No problems have been solved yet." I answer. "The streets are not full of people though. They're supposed to find another solution." I say. "You were supporting *Moosavi*?" he says. "I and many others voted for him to prove that it wouldn't make any difference."I say. "What if *Moosavi* was elected?" he says. "Then we could've controlled him and if nothing changed after four years, we'd vote for someone else to change. That's what elections are supposed to be for. It means that people must have the power to dismiss the one they've elected. Our goal is to change the constitution. It's not important who is president." I say. "Is there any money in writing books?" he says. "A writer doesn't write for money. There's a pain which makes a writer write. At the same time there can be lots of money in it too." I say. "How can I write a book?" he says. "Before writing you have to read books." I say.

"These guys do not know love. Just think about money. Life for these guys is synonymous with money. The craziest educational system in the world is to hide passion and love from school students. They are trying to destroy a nation by killing every kind of love." I say to my-self.

I greet the women from my mother's relatives outside the garden after the dinner. It's the first time I meet some of them. I also meet with the bride's grandmother, my mother's aunt. I kiss her forehead. All of my mother's aunts remind me of my grandmother. She passed away before the age of fifty when I was younger. Grandmothers usually play the role of the sun in the solar system. The family remains solid through their presence. After grandmother's death the family falls apart. Mr. *Naser* offers my mother and I a ride in his car. The rest join a ceremony regarding the bride. Sara, Hana, *Amir* and his wife set off for the ceremony. They give the bride and the groom a proper sendoff by joyriding on the streets and messing with each other and blocking the newlyweds' car. They won't let them go until the groom pays them. Despite what he wants, I take Ramtin with me.

In front of the newly wed couple's house we wait for them and others for an hour. Ramtin and I go to sleep in the car for an hour until their escorting operation comes to an end. I fall asleep at the bride's parents' place at around 3:30 after midnight and wake up in the next afternoon.

Raheleh Says: "one of the *Mr. Mehdi*'s relatives went to auntie last night and said that she wanted to Announce the Cheering for the new couple. I said that there was no need because my auntie was going to do it."

Mohsen says: "*Rodabeh* has called ten times since morning. She wants to come over but she feels shy."

Ms. Setareh turns towards me and says: "forgive me, I got busy with sewing and couldn't wait on you." "Please auntie I'm okey." I say. "You should have come and seen the bride's dowry. Setareh and Mr. Ali had done a lot." My mother tells me. "Lots of thanks to them." I reply. *Amir* says: "I want to go and get a signal light for Mr. *Mehdi*'s car today." "Why?" Setareh asks. "I crashed it last night." *Amir* answers. "Everyone was cutting off the others." Says Sara. "I actually got lucky. One slip-up and half of the car was gone." *Amir* adds. "What was going on last night?" I ask. "You should ask what wasn't!" Hana answers.

The women are preparing for a ceremony called *Patakhti*. It's customary for those who attend a wedding to go to the newlyweds' house with some gifts. This is how the bride's dowry is also presented.

I read a poem by *Fereydoon Moshiri*:

Curl your arm round my neck out of passion
Sprinkle the sky with the wine of your gaze
Allow me to look through the window of your eyes
At the moon's smile

I go to sleep. I watch some movies. *Samira* calls me and asks me to pour the beans she has soaked, in the pot and put it on the stove. The women and the girls come back home from *Patakhti* ceremony at 10:30pm. *Amir* and Hana and Sara and Hesam play cards. Ramtin and Raha and I also play cards. I am certain that our noises don't let the downstairs neighbor sleep.

Hana and *Amir* and *Sara* and I play cards after dinner. We bet on ice cream. Hana and I win the first hand. We lose the next. We lose again. We win another hand when we get 6 to 1. The smell of shisha has filled the place. We lose 7 to 2. "We won." I clap. "No we did." *Amir* says. "Then why are we celebrating?" I ask. Rafoneh looks at us confused. We go to bed at five in the morning.

The university entry exam results have been announced last night. I learn that Raheleh has been accepted majoring accounting. "If Raheleh takes the college seriously she'll be a competent manager." I say. "No benefit. They force each girl to marry. They do not let the girls go to work." Raheleh says with a quiet voice to hear me only. For the first time, we look at the eyes. "No girl is happy in this city. All the girls have a mask in their faces." she says with a slower sound than before. I look around. "In this city, every woman is a queen. But either in the palace of his father is imprisoned or in the palace of her husband." She says. Everyone is busy. She takes a mask again. "Do you drink tea?" She says loudly, with a smile. "Please in a big glass." I say, loudly.

Hana doesn't have her applicant's number, so she won't be able to check her results until we get home. I receive some texts from my underground students. They've thanked me for getting accepted into their favorite majors.

We go to auntie *Zahra* and Mr. *Naser*'s place. *Amir* and *Hana* and *Sara* and Shirin, *Amir*'s wife, play cards. *Ramtin* and Raha play with *Raha*'s toys. My mother talks with her aunt and I with Mr. Naser.

"Do you watch this talk show called Towards God?" he asks me. "No." I reply." "This man speaks so well. You should watch it for ten sessions. One session won't work. His thoughts relate to yours. Do you watch Joseph?" "No I don't watch TV." I say. "It became best film in the world. It was in the papers." he says. "I heard that the screenplay was stolen from its original writer." I say. "No you're not aware. These are just rumors. Just go and watch it. Have you seen Seven Sleepers of Ephesus?" he says. "No." I say. "Do you know what it's about?" he says. "I've read the story before." I say. "You should see the movie. The story isn't worth anything." he says. He is trying to find a way to brain-wahs me.

We go to *Koohsangi* in the evening. A mountain in the middle of the city. We sit on a rug around the corner. "They don't understand. Let's go have a walk." Mr. *Naser* tells me. He shows me almost the whole area. We climb the mountain. The stones are glowing in the moonlight. "The stones here are full of gold and silver. But extracting them costs too much. It's not worth it." He says. At the top there are eight anonymous martyrs buried. The information is written on a flag.

We sit down on the gravestones. People are coming and going. "Mom maybe this one is an Iraqi, how do we know?" A kid asks his mother. "We know by their soldier tags." She replies. "Do the children, who haven't seen the war, decide that there shouldn't be any more wars, or they get persuaded to it by looking at these tombs?" I think. I ask myself for what they were killed? I feel stuck amongst gears. I have lump in my throat. "This place got safe for families ever since these martyrs were buried here. Before that there were lots of thugs around here. Families wouldn't feel comfortable." Says Mr. *Naser*. We sit there for an hour. I close my eyes and lay myself down onto the universe. A slight breeze hits my face. "Let's get back." Says Mr. *Naser*. I look around.

Mashhad is surrounding us.

*****

Ramtin cries. "Where were you?" My mother asks. I smile. I embrace Ramtin. "I'm taking you to the amusement park." I say. I hold Raha and Ramtin's hands and we go to the playground. *Amir* also comes along.

73

Shirin, Amir's wife, reminds me the ice cream. "We don't usually grant the bet we lose." I say with smile.

Ramtin can't climb the rope in a vehicle. He always cries when he can't do something. "You're still too little son. A year later you can climb just like the other kids." "Then why these kids are climbing?" He asks. "Let's go to the slides."

"I hope his incapabilities always makes him cry." I think. "Every child in Middle East must learn to overcome their incapabilities." I say to Ramtin, I am sure he doesn't understand what I mean. He goes towards the tallest slide. There are no stairs. There's a ladder. The older kids clime over the younger ones. "Bravo. Good kids. The older look after the younger kids." I say. Ramtin would like me to watch him slide down. *Raha* joins.

Hana and *Amir* and I take a walk for an hour around the playground. "Dinner time." *Amir* looks at his cellphone and says. "They're going to have dinner." I convince Ramtin and Raha. I must promise to bring them back here after the dinner.

Rice with chicken and omelet. I choose omelet. "If the omelet isn't well-done, there's no ice cream for you." I say. Shirin puts them back on the stove. "I want eggs." Says Ramtin. "Have rice with chicken for now, I'll get you eggs tomorrow morning." I say. "I want eggs now." "We don't have eggs now. I'll make you tomorrow morning." Says my mother.

As promised, I take Ramtin to the playground after dinner. He gets tired in half an hour and we get back. Mr. *Naser* cuts some melon. "Cut properly and put them in the bowl for everyone." Says aunt *Zahra*. "No. I'll give everyone one big piece. It's more fun." Says Mr. *Naser*.

At home Amir prepares the shisha. He asks me to join. "You have your chat for now, I'm talking with Mr. *Neser*." I say. "Didn't you get tired of listening to my dad already?" Asks Khatoon. "No, he makes me talk actually." Answers Mr. *Naser*. "He doesn't say anything until the end when he says something that makes me start over." He says. "Khatoon took the day off to be with us." My mother says. "His father has allowed him to work in a women's barbershop." she says.

I look at Mr. *Naser*'s photo album. It's filled with letters of appreciation. Best of the year in *Basij*, successful operations, commanders' certificate of *Basij*, first place in shooting, ascending mount *Binaloud,* ascending mount *Sabalan*, letter of bravery...

"These are nothing. I didn't keep them all." He says. There are pictures of his youth when he had a textile factory in Tehran until war time. Then military maneuvers, rescue missions and .. .

"This is *Kordestan*." He shows me a picture. "Soon after the revolution I went to a village there. I asked all the people to come to the mosque. They gathered at the front door. I offered them to get in together. But no one did. One of them said that they couldn't because they weren't clean enough for they didn't have any showers there. Village houses had no bathroom. No water either. There were only one bathroom in the mosque. There was a small hole next to the toilet where there was water and they could wash up. Back then they would behead a Guard at night. When I asked them why they didn't do anything for it, they said that the government had to build them some bathrooms. You can't imagine. Now you must be thankful. You were born in a good time. You can be proud." He says. "You don't know the religion, or else you wouldn't talk like that." He adds. "What do you mean by religion?" I ask. "Like praying, charity and obedience to the leader." He says. "Why can't one be independent?" I ask. "Why no economical projects can take place without the presence of the masters and connected people to them? Which part of the religion says that a magazine permit must take eight years to be issued? Which part of the religion says that I must get a permit to publish a book? Which part of the religion says that in a such a rich country old people can have no pension or support? Why should I have to pass religious inquisitions to get hired in my own country? Why should I bribe everyone to live, to work, in my own country, in my own city?"

"Independent can't be." He says. "You have to depend on a place. To even produce soda they need to get permit from Standard Institute. You're unaware. You're mistaken." "This is not the way of running a country." I say. "We've invested in Lebanon and Iraq and Syria." He says. "At what cost? What do we get in return?" I ask. "You're mistaken. The decisions are not made individually." He says. "I know." I say. "No, you don't." He says. "My problem is not a specific person. My problem is lack of laws. The laws have been written wrongly in the last three decades, which is simply why all good achievements are denied now. The people are so oppressed that they're prepared to throw away these little achievements." I say. "Whose side are you taking?" He asks. "People's side. I'm a part of this people." I reply. "You're either on the side of Zionism or America. This is the enemy's talk." he says. "There are many people with different points of view around the world." I say. "It can't be." He says. "Do you know Hassan *Roshdieh*?" I say. "No." He answers. "He was son of a Mullah. Once, when hewas preaching, he said that if someone praises an oppressor, even by saying a few words, they would be an accomplice to all his crimes. Suddenly, *Mozaffareddin Mirza*, successor, entered the mosque. That moment *Roshdieh* changed his words and introduced the successor the justest of all. From that day on he never went to the mosque and quit being a Mullah. *Roshdieh* was the founder of contemporary schools in Iran. The believers would call him an infidel every time he built a school in every city. They broke his arm here in *Mashhad* and destroyed his school in *Tabriz*." I say. "Who destroyed the school?" He asks. "Theology students." I reply. "There are always spies amongst them to sabotage." He says. "If the laws are written correctly, they can be controlled. There are many people like *Hassan Reshdieh* in the world. Independent" I say.

— where are these things written?

— in books. In history.

— they write lies.

— any written thing can be a lie. There's no truth in the world.

"*Hassan Roshdieh* wasn't on anyone's side. He would be called an enemy if he was alive now." I say.

— You're one of those who aren't eligible to get any permit.

— Yes, I am. But why? Just because I am a secular man. I'd establish two schools in every city each year if it didn't depend on kneeling and begging and bribing the masters. But I learned my lessons after the first two schools and will never establish any organizations or firms.

— those many schools in our country, they belong to people.

— they don't belong to people. There's always one or some security forces among their board of directors.

—We can represent you a foreign company and you can make a good money in a short time.

I don't understand whether this is an attempted bribe or a kind offer. "I can sell my thoughts to the world. There's no need for me to become another's representative." I say.

"What are you after." He asks.

"I just want to live my life." I answer.

"You're responsible. If you demoralize someone, you're responsible." He says.

"God is satisfied with me. Because I'm moralizing his demoralized people." I say. "Whatever happens, those who have written contradictory laws are responsible."

"What do you want at end?" He asks. "A Secular Democratic Constitution based on popular vote." I say.

"They will stop you. They will kill you. What you want is impossible. That's why there are a lot of problems for you and your family. I know everything about you. Your former colleagues are all working for us. All of them. You cannot do anything in education again. You are alone. There is no friend for you. Do you want to regime change by your-self?" He says. "My son was taken hostage for two years, but now he is with me. I was supposed to not live, but I survived. I'm sure the situation will change in our favor. As you know, I came back from death, that's why I'm not afraid of anything." I say.

Hana jumps out of the room. "I won." She says loudly. "I lost a shisha." *Amir* rubs his forehead and says. Ramtin at one corner and Raha at the other are sleeping. I go to the room where everyone is sitting. I get waited on with a cup of tea. I get a puff of the shisha. What were you talking about?" *Amir* asks. "Just having a conversation." I answer. "My dad is an important man. Sometimes they come after him with bodyguards." He says. "I see. He himself is the Islamic Republic." I say. He laughs. I go to buy ice cream along with Sara and Hana and *Amir* and Khatoon. *Shirazi* ice cream for six people, and *Kermani* ice cream for five. *Amir* buys *Rana* a shisha. I get normal ice cream for Ramtin and Raha.

"I'll go to sleep." Sahar says around dawn. "Let's look and find Khatoon a job tomorrow morning, because I don't think she can stay awake at work tomorrow." I say. Khatoon laughs under the chador. I look at the time. I hope I could convince Mr. Naser that I and we are not the enemy, that enemy is hiding within his and his like-minded people's thoughts. I know that he will reflect on it a couple of days after we leave *Mashhad.*

We're invited to my mother's other aunt's place the next noon. Mr. *Akbar*, aunt Akram's husband, is sick. They say he's had an incomplete stroke. We go to their place along with aunt *Zahra*. Mr. *Akbar* has his usual smile on his face and a white coif on his head. "God keep sickness away *haji Akbar.*" I say. He laughs. "It's his fault." Says aunt *Zahra*. "We were going on a holiday to North. The same morning *Khosrow* came over. I told Mr. *Akbar* to tell him that we were going on a holiday. He didn't. But I told him to stay with *Khosrow*. The kids and I left. Then they went to *Neyshabour* where Mr. *Akbar* came down." She continues. I look at Mr. *Akbar*. He smiles.

"They had a bachelor time and that's what he got." Says aunt *Zahra*.

"I didn't fast. But Mr. *Akbar* wouldn't listen. *Ramadan* has weakened him." Says aunt *Akram*.

"You should be more careful Mr. *Akbar*. We're not young anymore." Says aunt *Zahra*.

Mr. *Akbar* cuts a pear and gets closer to me. "My dear, after years *Khosrow* has come to *Mashhad* from England. He's looked for a hotel but couldn't find any empty room because since it's after *Ramadan* everyone has traveled to here. Then he's come over to our place. I can't throw my guest out. It's impossible. No matter how many times I tell her, she doesn't listen. I begged the kids. I had them call their mom and let her know. You can't imagine how she made my body shiver in front of *Khosrow* that day. Now she says it's because of *Ramadan*. It's all because of my boiling blood. She drove me up the wall that day. I'm not young anymore. I can't. A simple thing can make me drop. But who'd understand." He says.

"Take it easy *haji*." I say. "I know my dear. I just opened my heart." He answers.

The subtitle news on a satellite TV reads Turkish prime minister, during his trip to Egypt, has said that the uniting motto of Muslims must be human rights and democracy.

Kookoo sabzi, chicken fried chunks, fesenjoon, gheime, rice, yogurt and salad Prepared for lunch. A full hospitality in Iranian style.

"I want lots of lemon." Says Ramtin at lunch. "Have some vinegar." I show him the apple vinegar." I get half a spoon vinegar close to his mouth. He shivers for

some moments. "You'll get an ice cream this evening if you finish your food." I say. He pours half of his food in my plate.

The bus leaves for Karaj at 8:30 with an hour delay. Before leaving the bus station, the driver asks me and some other passengers to get off. I ask for the reason. "Our bus has four extra seats. For each extra passenger we have to pay 3000 *Tomans* of tax." They say. It takes half an hour to get passed the pay toll. "What kind of law can be traded for money?" I think. I take a look at the front facade of the bus station. It's written: "the Islamic awakening in the Middle Eastern countries is a result of the Islamic Republic in Iran."

There is a movie on the display of the bus which couldn't get screening and publishing permit when it was produced. Its disks got distributed on the streets by the street venders.

"The story of traveling to Mashhad which I'm going to write, will be completed with the movie *Santouri*." I think.

Whatever I was trying to tell Mr. *Naser,* is properly told the oppressors and angels in black by *Dariush Mehrjouyi* in this movie.

I watch the news on *Al Arabiya* channel when I get home. The Turkish prime minister has told the Egyptian youngsters that a laic government isn't without religion and they shouldn't be afraid of forming one. The Muslim Brotherhood hasn't liked that saying of the Turkish prime minister. The other channel is showing a moving skeleton who has lots of flies on his head and his mother's black breasts are dry and dangling. Mother gazes at my eye with her sparkling eyes.

"I'm hungry." Says Ramtin. "What would you like to eat?" I ask him. "Lift me up so I'd see what's in the fridge." He says. "Cheese, butter, lots of lemon, grapes, cookies." He says.

Hana says that she's been accepted to major in Natural Resources Engineering. "Will you enroll?" I ask. "I only want to major in Medicine. I'll study for the next year." Answers she. "My publisher has told me to go there tomorrow and sign the last copy before issuing." Says Sara.

"Great." I say. I log in to my email; It takes a long time. Darya has emailed and asked me to send her in Afghanistan my last written book. I write to her that I want to consult with her about my newest book.

"I've invited auntie and Mr. *Naser* and *Amir's* family to come over to our house." Says my mother. "With pleasures." I say. "They will come months later." She says. "The kids had lots of fun. We should have them have fun the next time as well." I say. "I think Raheleh likes you. Do you want to marry her?" she says. "You are wrong. I do not think she is looking for a husband. She is looking for freedom. I'm not looking for a stepmother for my son, too. I wish my life was as simple as you imagine Mom." I say. "I am a mother. I want you to be happy."

She says. "How can I be happy when others are suffering." I say. "Be like everyone else, live the life." She says. "The rest do not live. They are just alive." I say.

About Translator

Bijan Safshekan was born in Shiraz, a city in south of Iran, in July 3rd 1986. He is an English teacher, translator and interpreter, currently living in middle of Turkey.

Graduating from Dramatic Arts high school, he started his English career by majoring in English Translation at the University of Shiraz in September 2006.

Meanwhile though, since the beginning of high school in 2001, he took part in many theatrical projects for both children and adults as an actor. His translation life got more serious after he graduated from the university and moved to Tehran in 2010. He translated many articles in many different fields for university students both from English to Persian and from Persian to English. Knowing how to work with editing softwares from his past experience, he subtitled some short movies in order for them to participate in international festivals. Simultaneously he used to work for several language schools and institutions as part time English conversation and proficiency teacher throughout Tehran. He also was involved in some simultaneous interpretation projects, one of which was for Fajr International Film Festival where he was to interpret for Mr. Brian Dooley from Canada at his professional Mask Acting workshop.

Eventually in January 2014, he moved to Turkey along with his wife and has been working as an English teacher ever since, until recently that he translated some poems and short stories to English and finally his first book "A Knuckle-Deep Ocean".

About Author's

'Babak Esmaeily' was initially a pen name for an author who wanted to start writing and publishing books at the age 40. However, due to couple of life circumstances his path changed.

Babak was born in Iran in 1975 and lived there as an executive director of a multi-purpose institution, Director of Education, educational counselor and a math teacher, as well as editor in chief of a training journal which was released every two weeks for student, parents, and teachers. While he lived in Iran, Babak attended hundreds of libraries and schools as a lecturer: How to Read a Book.

When he was 30, something happened. Babak's linguistic ability to understand what happened was not enough. There was a complexity; a chaos in its scientific sense. The severity of the damage was so high that he could not talk about it.

When you encounter a complexity, it is necessary to decompose it into its constructive components. The discovery of all the truth does not happen on one occasion. The pieces of it must be found and glued together. Once you have found all the truth, you cannot offer it, but you must leave it to rest in the same way that you found it. The pieces of it must be put up in different places, so if anyone is interested in finding the truth, they go the same way that you've gone. As soon as the truth is found it disappears, because text does not have the same meaning for audiences.

So far, Babak's works published in Persian are focused on truth finding.

A knuckle-Deep Ocean is Babak's first work translated into English. It is not the whole truth, but just an introduction to it.

The Savior in the Mirror, Golchehreh, and *Rainbow Lady* are being translated and will be published in the future. All these books have been written in the ten years that Babak was trying to change misfortune into blessing.

After five years of *Living in the Center of the Earth* in Turkey, now Babak is living in the United States, *The Country of Appointments.*

Printed in the United States
By Bookmasters